Viv Booth was born in Oldham in 1957, the youngest of four children. Move forward fifty years and you have the meanderings of a short, slightly overweight, middle aged woman living in France, predominantly alone. Not a totally uncommon occurrence but pretty damn unusual for a Lancashire lass.

I would like to dedicate this book to my husband Martyn,
thank you for letting me be me.

Viv Booth

PAYING WITH FISH

AUSTIN MACAULEY PUBLISHERS™

LONDON • CAMBRIDGE • NEW YORK • SHARJAH

A CIP catalogue record for this title is available from the British Library.

ISBN 9781398436404 (Paperback)
ISBN 9781398436411 (ePub e-book)

www.austinmacauley.com

First Published 2022
Austin Macauley Publishers Ltd®
1 Canada Square
Canary Wharf
London
E14 5AA

Thank you to all my family and friends, old and new, for their support and who define this book. Without you there would be no story.

Vous Avez Choisi?

Friday, 28 January

If we are going to live in France, I am going to have to learn some more French.

I am one of those people who think that if you are in a foreign country, you should immerse yourself in their culture, customs and language. I laugh at Karl Pilkington in 'An Idiot Abroad' for all the right reasons but also because in my haughty self-assured pontificating, I think to myself, *I am just not going to be like that*. Well, that is okay up to a point. It is fine when you are sat at home in your cosy English speaking environment, sounding very smug and probably very annoying, watching some poor man being made to ride a bucking bronco but it is a totally different thing when you get here.

The French must think I sound like a blithering idiot.

Cecil, our son-in-law, once told us that he had never been to France, only Paris. We thought this was hilarious in our 'oh, so superior', conceited, we are so sophisticated manner.

He was right.

There is a world of difference between having a romantic weekend in Paris or a holiday in Normandy than having a house hunting expedition in Brittany. When we arrived here in Brest in the early evening, we decided we would venture up the main high street to find somewhere to eat. There did not seem to be many restaurants to choose from, mainly shops, but it was because we were probably referencing the British high street and not the French. Eventually, we did find one that we liked the look of and after a childish exercise of pushing and shoving each other while shouting 'you go first', 'no, you go first', 'no, you go first', we finally bundled unceremoniously together through the door whilst giggling and glaring at each other in equal measures.

We managed to muster up enough decorum and ask for a table and mustered a 'No' when asked aloofly if we had made a reservation. With a typical Gallic shrug and a bit of a huff we were led to a table by a waiter with the air about him of 'Oh, we've got a right pair here'.

This is when we realised we were in a different France. There was not a word of English on the menu and none of the words appeared to be those we had learned a long time ago in the Language Lab. All our 'oh, we are not typical English men abroad' attitude went out the window. It was a little bit of a blow to my self-esteem when reflecting later that I honestly thought there would be translation line underneath each selection on the menu, like there was when we went on package holidays to Spain, Greece and Italy. We were well-travelled you know.

We could not make head nor tail of it. We both poured over it, repeated parts of it out loud to ourselves and each other but it was no good, not a clue. At this point, when I thought we would have to slope off unseen and head for McDonald's (which would be highly unlikely as most of the diners in the restaurant had been watching us intently since we first fell indoors), I noticed a chalk board advertising *Plat du jour*. Well, I knew what that meant and I was not bothered what it would consist of. At least we could order it and have something to eat. But as luck would have it said, it was *Porc Curry*. Practically the same spelling, thank goodness for that.

Saturday, 29 January

Morning

Today was our first day house hunting in France.

I had scoured the internet previously and I feel I knew every house that was available within our small budget for sale in Brittany. We only have £40,000 to play with, which in the UK is a small amount but in France today with the exchange rate of one Euro equalling 66 pence coupled with the cheapness and the availability of potential properties, we felt we would get something. There is an added pressure of trying to find something when you are in this situation though because it is not like trying to buy somewhere at home where you have the luxury of viewing properties over weeks or even months. House hunting in France feels more intense due to time and money constraints surrounding work and travel. However, there are definite plus points because as it is going to be a 'holiday home', there are not the same emotional considerations attached and let us be frank, it is quite exciting.

We had decided that we could not afford anything by the sea as coastal properties tend to be more expensive and we did not want a new property, like many of the Brits moving to France, we wanted an old, typical French property. Which is lucky for us really, as there are many available due to the fact that young French people want brand new houses, usually in the cities but even in the countryside they definitely want new builds, not 'Maison's ancient'. Many of the old houses available have been passed down through the families and are being sold either because there is no one left alive or more commonly that the younger family members have moved away.

Over a period of time we had viewed numerous properties on the internet – a very relaxing and pleasant pastime had narrowed them down to our 'favourites' and so had been in touch with three French estate agents. Today we were seeing a house in Uzel in the morning, represented by one estate agent and then two houses in Perret and Bothoa in the afternoon being marketed by a different realtor. We had arranged to meet Alain at the first *immobilier* in Loudeac this morning.

Online research stated that Loudeac is a pretty market town with many traditional buildings and mediaeval streets to enjoy with a population of just over 9,000. We had made the journey here from Brest in Finistere as we had never been to this part of France. We were unsure of the locations of hotels and we had heard that French hotels were not very good, so we have played it safe by staying at a Holiday Inn, big wusses, therefore, it has taken us two hours to reach the first of our destinations. We found a car park and made our way towards the first agents which we had located as we did a quick drive around the town before we parked. I did not really notice the type and history of the buildings as described in our research as it faded into the background as we first encountered the strange custom of piped music played in the streets. At first we thought that perhaps it was being played for a special occasion, for a fete or a market or something, but we quickly came to realise that this was not the case. This was just normal Saturday morning activity. It was like being on the set of The Prisoner.

It was, therefore, that the receptionist was met with the presence of two wide-eyed English people at her desk. When you are in the relative safe environment of a school classroom with your fellow classmates and tutor, practicing your French, it does seem moderately easy but when you are faced with a living, breathing real French person, it is a whole different matter. And in no way does 'where is my aunt's hat' and 'the monkey is in the tree' equip you for a real-life conversational situation. Let alone one that includes uncommon English words such as conveyancing.

We did the best we could and we said in our best French, "We come see house."

Luckily, the receptionist was ready for us. I believe it was quite an uncommon occurrence to have two English house hunters in the office on a Saturday morning. She explained to us that Alain was the estate agent who was going to show us the house and called to the said homme. It is strange but both Mr C and I are the same. We cannot speak a great deal of French, lack of confidence on my part being a large contributory factor but we can understand a vast amount. We, therefore, understood that we were going to view the house that we had seen in Uzel first but there was another house that had come onto the market in the same area and did we want to view that one? We acceded but between ourselves we did feel it was above our budget.

We made our way to Uzel in Alain's car. Mr C sat in the front with myself in the back. We tried our best to communicate and did even achieve a little 'chit chat'. Well, it was mostly Alain speaking and us trying to glean some information buried within the unbelievably fast spoken French.

It has to be said that there are a lot of similarities in France and the UK, although many people would have you believe otherwise, but it was our experience that some things are the same the world over, Estate Agent photographs of houses for sale being one of them. Unfortunately, the photos on the internet were of the outside only, which did in some instances resemble what stood before us but did not reveal that the house was down an alleyway behind a wool shop. The house was a two-bedroomed detached, which we knew, but the only outside space was a small walled garden at the front.

I mustered all my knowledge of the French language at my disposal and asked, "The garden facing south?"

Alain appeared to understand what I had said as he responded immediately with "Good question", looking at me with approval, considered the question and then replied, "I don't know."

We entered the front door straight into a lounge, which was the only room on that floor but I was not prepared for the French people's taste in oversized dark wood furniture. It was coupled with a staircase in the corner going up a floor and down a floor and an enormous deeply ornate drinks bar in the opposite corner. It all made me feel a little like Alice through the Looking Glass.

Firstly, we went downstairs to the kitchen, which was not fully fitted but again filled with very rustic large standalone furniture and an old sink in the corner and I had a sneaky suspicion that there was woodworm in those beams the amount of dust that was lying around. Following this, we made our way up two sets of stairs to the bedroom floor. The theme of the oversized furniture continued up here but the bathroom was a sight to behold and was an assault on my over wrought senses. The bathroom suite itself was orange but it was not just one shade of this extremely striking colour but an ensemble of differing hues, dark to light, filtering down the porcelain. If this delight was not enough, the wallpaper sealed the vision before us. It was red, white, turquoise and lime green in colour with the pattern resembling a multitude of Hawaiian shirts pasted to the walls for our enchantment.

Needless to say, this was not the house of our dreams and so we went to view the house that Alain had suggested. When we entered through the front door, covered by a shattered glass canopy, I became to realise the style of furniture in the other house was standard French décor and wallpaper. They just love it and the more clashing colour and patterns involved, the better. This house was not for us either. The slightly terrifying 'chucky' like doll that was sat rather menacingly on the double bed did not add to the allure but evil spirits would be warded off by the proximity of the house to the church, facing it in fact. However, the downside of the chiming of bells at seven o'clock on a Sunday morning cancelled that out. The clincher that made me realise I would not be running headlong into purchasing this gem was the old shirt pegged on a frayed washing line in the attic, surrounded by a multitude of dead mice.

Afternoon

We drove from Loudeac and the rotting mammals towards Bothoa and Perret to view our next two houses advertised through a different estate agent based near the first property in Bothoa. When I say based near, it was in the middle of nowhere, as you seem to find in France. All that was there surrounded by fields was a Boulangerie, a car park and the estate agents. Of course, we had not timed it correctly and we arrived during the lunch hour. Well, I use that term loosely because they take two hours and more for their midday break.

We sat patiently in the car park to await the return of the agents, which they did at about 14.40 and we strode into the building, outwardly a lot more confidently than we felt. However, the agents knew some English and again we were a bit of a rarity, so they knew why we were there and which houses we wanted to view, which did not tax our grasp of French too much. The next bit did, however. It took a long time for the agents to explain and for us to understand, our fault completely, it has to be said, no one would be accompanying us to the viewings. We were to be let loose alone. Once the agents were happy we had comprehended what they were saying, they handed over two enormous brass keys, one for each property and waved us dismissively out of the premises.

We left with reluctance and not a little confused, as we had no idea how to get to the houses. I am, it has to be said, a fair map reader but we had gleaned in the melee that was the conversation in the agent's premises, that although the second house was in Bothoa, the first was not in Perret but in a tiny hamlet nearby. This was going to severely test my orienteering skills.

On the internet the first house on our list looked like a little castle, perched securely atop of a hill.

Yes, it is up a hill, a dirty great big winding and mountain. Well, not a mountain exactly, but a flipping big mound. We struggled at first to identify the house because when we eventually managed to find the hamlet with our meagre understanding of the directions, it appeared to be a series of farm buildings with no singular spectacular edifice to be seen. Further investigation into the courtyard of the said farm buildings revealed our quest, for sat in the corner betwixt a cow shed and a stable, was 'the' castle. It was basically a two up and down double fronted tiny-terraced house with a rounded wall and a turret. We did not even enter, utilising the impressive brass key as one look through the glassless windows was enough. We scurried back into the hire car, watched closely by a very curious red-faced farm worker. We then tried to manoeuvre out of the courtyard while giggling uncontrollably about how we could not bring a bunch of hormonal teenagers up a mountain in rural France for a holiday in farm building.

Engineering the descent down the hill from the house was hampered slightly by the small turning circle abutted by hay and cow muck and the sheer indifference to his own mortal safety by the labourer, who refused to move from his vantage point. Our journey away once started was further impeded by a surly looking dog, which insisted on walking down the middle of the one-track road at a palatial pace while throwing his enormous penis from side to side, slapping the middle of his back, creating a fascinating metronome effect on our now hysterically laughing spirits.

It was clear once we had managed to overtake the well-endowed canine that the house was not the Englishman's little castle in France and although I had laughed until my sides hurt, I was beginning to think we were never going to find anything. One thing for sure was that it could not get any weirder.

Wrong.

Bothoa was located quite easily in comparison to the last location and although there are houses there, again the second viewing was not in the town but in a hamlet on the outskirts. The details on the internet had described it as *Maison de Maitre*, which literally translated means 'Master's House'. They are usually large, impressive houses with a central door and rooms on either side of the hall, normally four rooms downstairs and four on the first floor, many do have a second-floor attic. The picture displayed for our viewing was a very impressive photograph of the outside façade with no further pictures as we were finding the usual practice, so far, of the inside.

We located the house immediately as it was the only one of that type in the village. There was a convenient car park facing it but I was a little disconcerted when I realised that the main purpose for the handy parking facility was in fact to serve the graveyard adjacent. The house was situated directly opposite with a large imposing door opening straight onto the road itself. I say opening, it took some great skill and not a little strength by Mr C to access this portal with the enormous brass key provided due to the fact it had quite obviously been closed for some time.

We bundled unceremoniously into the hall, that had an impressive, if worn and dusty staircase placed directly in front of us. We started to creep around the hall to the room directly to our left. We were tiptoeing and whispering as we went, as if we were perhaps not meant to be in there, even though we had the key. We peered through the door into what was allegedly the kitchen. We had got used to traditional French kitchens by now, the sink in the corner, no fitted cupboards and a rabble of mis-matched seemingly random furniture but added to this one was the dirt, the obligatory dead mice and the most overbearingly awful smell. This pungency was gingerly investigated to reveal a door in the corner, hiding a visible but not odourlessly disguised earth toilet. Disgusting.

Across the hall, which we traversed in the same unique manner as before, was another room, thus totalling two on the ground floor. Before we entered, we imagined it was going to be a grand 'salon', it was indeed a multifunctional room but it seemed to be a lounge crossed with a bedroom. How did we determined this? I have no idea as there were no clues to the usage other than a dirty mattress on the floor and a bicycle parked against a wall. This space was again rodent infested and filthy.

We decided to mount the stairs and investigate the next floor. We were still being very quiet and looking suspiciously into corners. I, however, had developed a further unusual characteristic of crouching low, not unlike Groucho Marx with every one of my senses on high alert. Mr C was already in the room to the right at the top of the stairs due to the tardiness and unusual gait to my ascent and was awaiting my arrival. As I entered headfirst, body following after, I espied a large dark wood unit, not dis-similar to a sideboard and on top of it was placed a partly inscribed gravestone dated 1966.

Well, I was off.

Gone was the creeping and the whispering. I was running; not only was I running, but I was also screaming and laughing hysterically at the same time. I tumbled headlong out of the door into the street, just managing to keep my footing and I did not give a backward glance until I was out of there. I just did not care. It was like the devil was snapping at my heels.

Thank goodness it was a sleepy little hamlet and there was no traffic around, otherwise I could have been crushed under the wheels of a 2CV but I did not care and by the time Mr C came out of the entrance, wondering where the hell I was, I was at the back of the car park as far away as possible.

What a great day, I have never laughed or enjoyed house hunting so much before in my life.

Sunday, 30 January

Today was our second day of house viewing.

We did wonder after yesterday's enjoyable but fruitless search if we were ever indeed going to find our dream house in France? May be our expectations are too high for the budget we have got.

A little negotiation had to be performed to actually view any house on a Sunday as Estate Agents and many other shops, other than the obligatory Boulangerie, are closed on the Sabbath. However, luckily for us the man who was showing us around the two properties we had shortlisted was English and so was quite happy to work when his colleagues were in church or not as the case may be.

Originally, we had identified a sixteenth-century town house in the centre of Morlaix as the house we wanted to view, unfortunately, a week before we were due to arrive, it was taken off the market. However, there was an apartment in the centre of the town within our budget, which, Stan, the agent, thought we would like.

Morlaix is a large town known for sixteenth-century houses, cobbled streets and the enormous viaduct along the *Quai de Leon*, which was built using local pink granite in the nineteenth century to facilitate the movement of trains between Rennes and Brest.

We had arranged to meet Stan at the bandstand in front of the Hotel de Ville, a clearly identifiable landmark in the middle of the town just behind the viaduct. Luckily, there is a car park practically next to it, so we did not have to do too much traffic negotiation to locate Stan already waiting for us. It was a short walk across the road to the apartment he wished us to view. It was a little bit of a shock to realise that the object of our outing was located behind a nondescript door between a shoe shop and a winery. It really did not match our 'roses around the door' view of our ideal second home.

When we entered the flat after climbing three sets of steep stairs, enough to put us off in itself, the interior did not disappoint our now common view point that French homeowners are completely bonkers mad. They just do not seem to care about the appearance of their homes. The majority of English sellers would at least try and present their home in some form of order.

The flat consisted of three unfurnished rooms, a lounge/diner/kitchen, a bathroom and a bedroom. It was not necessarily empty. There were old clothes, rubbish and newspaper strewn across all the floors. It must have been a business at some point, a solicitor or some such enterprise as there was an array of cupboards, containing a variety of different sized pigeonholes along one wall, which supported this theory and a wall covered in pretend brick wallpaper, peeling at the edges. There was no outside space, which if it had been the most immaculate, wonderful, beautiful apartment, it would have ruled it out but the 'piece de resistance' was the dirty great big four-foot hole in the middle of the floor.

This was not our dream, more like a mini nightmare!

We had one more roll of the dice, one more property to view before Stan went to do whatever he normally did on a Sunday and we went back to Brest to prepare to return to the UK.

The week before we had set off for the house hunt in France, Stan had contacted us by e-mail to say that an apartment had just come on the books. It was not on the internet as yet, so there was no description or interior photos. However, he had been there and had taken a photograph out of the kitchen window to try and illustrate the proximity of the property to the beach. Unfortunately, the day that he took it was inclement and all that could be seen was a lot of grey. Would we like to view it? Why not?

The apartment was located in a little seaside village called Primel Tregastel.

On the way to the village, a journey of approximately 15 minutes, we were following Stan in our car. We were discussing our expectations, budget, disappointment and the fun we had had trying to find a second home and how we were not expecting too much on this occasion also.

At this point we traversed the roundabout at the commencement of the descent into Primel Tregastal and just at that moment the sun peeped out from behind a cloud and there and then I experienced 'the dream' for there was the most enchanting visage played out in front of us. As the road wound downhill, pretty little houses nestled amongst the abundant pine trees, revealing shimmering glimpses of water and boats at regular intervals along the way, culminating in a picturesque harbour with sun kissed boats bobbing in the sea surrounded at random points by jutting, granite rock formations. It was just quite magical.

"Now don't get too excited." Warned Mr C.

"What do you mean?" I replied, knowing full well what he was talking about, this was seemingly a little too good to be true.

"Well, you need to be calm." He reasoned. "If you like it when we get in, don't let Stan know. We need to negotiate a good price if we want it and we don't want him to think we are over eager."

He knows me so well. He knew that I had immediately fallen in love with the place and may be my personal dream of living near the sea was possibly going to become a reality.

As we followed the road around to the right, we entered the main street, Rue le Grand Large, which in turn led directly onto the sea front but our destination was on the right-hand side near the bottom of the street. As we parked outside the building, I tried to absorb as much about the outside as I could.

The building was two storeys with a door at each end of the ground floor, sandwiching between them four-shuttered windows. The top floor displayed five further shuttered windows, three belonging to the apartment we were to view and two owned by the adjacent flat. The ground floor had a sign above the windows declaring the establishment to be a grocer's, which of course was closed it being a Sunday. To the left, adjoined to the shop was a single storey bar, *Le Boujaron,* which too was not open and across the full width of both establishments was a wooden deck which stopped at the side of the second, right hand door. To the right of the block was a drive and a single storey restaurant, *Au Gouter Breton*.

We entered the building through the right-hand glass door into a long, narrow hallway, where at the end were a couple of stairs turning into an unseen staircase leading up to the two apartments. On the left-hand side running the full length of the hall was a low wall filled with plastic plants and behind it a full-length wall to ceiling mirror. It was like walking into a 1970s' nightclub without the ambient light and disco ball. We mounted the stairs to find a small landing with a tiny window on the right and two doors on the left, our viewing was behind the second door.

If the door was anything to go by, it was not going to be too promising. However, as we entered the flat, there was a pleasant surprise. It was full of light streaming in. This was because it was mainly one big lounge/diner/kitchen but there were four windows and a set of patio doors in that room alone. In addition to the main room, there was a bathroom, a bedroom and in the corner of the principal room a staircase leading to a mezzanine floor which ran the full length of the apartment. It was like a French take on a New York loft but with smaller proportions.

There was definitely cosmetic work to be done. The bathroom was old-fashioned but clean. The kitchen, if you could call it that, consisted of a sink and two wall cupboards, that did not bother me as I was now getting used to the French version of the 'cuisine'. The main room had a wooden floor which was good with the remainder of the surfaces covered in a cheap foam backed carpet of an indiscriminate colour.

I loved it!

I only just stopped myself screeching out loud with glee when I saw the longed-for fantasy view out of both kitchen windows. If Mr C was to pick me up and throw me, I would have landed in the sea.

We continued to look around with Stan and when the viewing came to an end, we were very non-committal about our views on the property and whether we wanted to progress. As we descended the stairs and returned to the street, we were calmness personified when we explained that we would just stay a little while longer and look around the village.

As Stan drove away and we walked down the street as if being pulled by an unseen magnetic force towards the shore, Mr C looked at me with confusion and incredulity shining in his eyes and said a little accusingly, "Well, you were very quiet in there and you didn't seem to get excited at all."

"Well, you told me not to," I responded indignantly.

Saturday, 17 June

Well, we have bought it.

We put an offer in when we got back home and after a little negotiation it was accepted. Hooray! Of course, the buying process in France is not the same as in the UK as you would expect. We employed a French speaking solicitor at home. I know that a lot of people buying in France do not do that but as our French language skills are so limited around the terminology associated with all conveyancing matters, we decided that it was the best option. Luckily because we were back at home when we made the offer, we did not have to fill in an offer *d'achat,* however, even though it was a verbal offer all the legal terms and conditions applied and both ourselves and the vender had a seven-day cooling off period to decide whether we really did want to buy or indeed she wanted to sell. Once that period was over, the real contract stuff began. The vender chooses the *notaire* and estate agents and you, as the buyer, have to pay for both of these agencies' fees – a bit different than in the UK! These fees can be about 12% of the asking price, so quite steep really. Once a *Compromis de vente* has been signed, which we did through power of attorney, there is no going back. Well, there is, of course, but if either the buyer or seller reneges they have to pay the other 10% of the purchase price. Blimey!

It is ours!

The problem or not if you love to shop of a second home, which I did not really think about, is that you have nothing to put in it. We managed to find spare knives and forks and stuff like that at home but we needed beds, cooker, washer, sofas, etc. etc. To be honest, as we were not sure of the furniture shops in France, we bought most of that type of thing at home but we knew we would have to brave the electrical shops for white goods etc. because of the different voltage. Hey, ho, that should be interesting, sat conjugating lists of verbs at senior school was not going to help us there.

We moved what furniture we have into the apartment yesterday. I could not wait to move in but even though we are cash buyers, it still took four months to go through all the rigmarole of the legal stuff but now we are here. Getting two sofas up the stairs on our own was very challenging and at one point, I literally could not move, not only because I was having a fit of the giggles but also as it was a physical impossibility as my head was wedged between a sofa and the side of the staircase. But we did it. We were a little

26

disappointed when we first entered the flat to find that the vendor had covered up the lovely floorboards in the lounge with cheap stick-on pretend parquet floor tiles but even so, we were both very excited to be here and that was something we could sort out over time.

However, there was one thing we could not correct. We had no water. We did not even know where the water connection was, never mind, anything else. We searched in all the predictable places but no luck. We managed to contact the estate agents and they got in touch with the vendor but she lived in Nantes and had got the keys for the stop cock there, so her poor dad had to drive there, retrieve them and bring them back to us. In the meantime, Mr C decided that as we had no idea how long that would take, we would book into a hotel.

I do not know if you have ever been in a French hotel but they do not really seem to do them very well. This could, of course, just be our personal experience. There were no hotels in our village or those close by, so we decided to go to Morlaix as surely there would be some there. Yes, there are two, one definitely did not look too good, so we plumped for the second one right in the centre near the rendezvous bandstand, The Hotel L'Europe. It states in the promotional literature that the hotel has been there for 200 years.

Yes, it felt like it.

Also, that the original décor will take you back in time and is an invitation to relax in comfort.

Er, no.

Best of all that it has a majestic staircase.

Yes, but threadbare.

And luxury, comfortable rooms.

Oh, my life! We were up in the attic, the bed, which sagged in the middle was covered with a candlewick bedspread and seemed to be miles away from the seemingly 200-year-old television set perched on top of the enormous, elaborately decorated wardrobe. The carpet, well, what can I say, do not take off your shoes or you may extend your stay there for longer than you expected and may need a crowbar to unstick your feet. But the best bit by far was the bathroom. I just fell about laughing when I saw it. It was not so much that it did not have a solid wall. The top of the said partition appeared to be constructed with what can only be described as stair rods. It was the fact that I would need a step ladder to get into the bath and had no idea how I would ever get out again without the help of Mr C.

Tuesday, 26 July

In at the deep end, I think.

I am here on my own for the first time. Well, I am not exactly on my own. I have the two girls, Jemima and Daphne, with me. I might as well be on my own when it comes to speaking to the locals as their grasp of the French language is limited to say the least. They both did some French at school but both preferred German, not much help for me here and although they have both been on holiday in France several times, it is definitely not the same as living in a village where we are the only English residents. They do try it has to be fair but not with very good results, well, they do not try at all really, hence the milk incident.

We had been here a couple of days and the only person we have seen to converse with is Madame de Bonvillier, who owns the apartment next door. She does not live there but rents it out as a summer holiday let, as yet we have not seen any tenants but we have only been here a few days. I think we missed them on the change-over. I did not, however, miss Madame de Bonvillier.

I feel as though I have to give her full title each time I mention her, as apparently if your name contains 'de', it means you are descendent from royalty. She did not tell me her name, I gleaned it from the label on her post box. She looks to be in her 80s. I know that she used to live in Paris and that she used to be a television journalist. How I know these details I have no idea. I seem to learn things here by a process of osmosis, I just do not know how they get in there! There is a certain arrogance about some French people in particular. I do not know whether it was a result of her ancestors having their heads chopped off or the fact that she hails from Paris but Madame de Bonvillier definitely has it.

When I say that I converse with her, that is stretching the truth a little to say the least. It is more like she gives me an order and I accept it, no questions asked. The first time I met her was when she was on the stairs with her friend. This *ami* seemed to have the sole purpose of cleaning the flat whilst smoking an obscene number of cigarettes. She always has one on the go, hanging out of the side of her mouth, she appeared to be in her 80s also. When I met them, I was told in no uncertain manner that I should always keep the front door double locked. There were no circumstances that negated this activity. She said it very politely after the normal *bonjours* but it was quite clear to me that this request was to be obeyed. There is no consideration on her part that I am English and that I may not understand. I am told and I should do it and that is that.

Not long after this rendezvous I realised we had run out of milk and asked Jemima to nip down to the grocers below to fetch some, very handy that. Jemima is at an age where she is not concerned whether see looks a bit of a berk when trying a foreign language. It is either that or it is the arrogance of youth and she will just speak English no matter what. I honestly think it is the latter.

On entering the shop, she said her 'bonjour' and then stated in an enquiring voice to nice gentleman owner Alain, "Milk." No more no less.

Alain did not appear to be put out by this request and replied, "Lait."

Jemima a little confused replied, "Milk."

"Lait," came the response.

This exchange of single words went on for some time until Alain out of desperation, I presume, kept repeating both words with the emphasis on lait until the penny dropped.

These two conversations, well, they can hardly be called that are the only two interchanges I have had with French people since we arrived three days ago and are hardly going to help me out of the predicament I am in at the moment; my phone will not work.

Wednesday, 27 July

Note to self-phone companies are bloody idiots.

We do not have a landline in the apartment, partly because we have only just got the flat but more truthfully because we do not really know the process of getting one, so I have been relying on my mobile phone for communication with Mr C in the UK. This was fine at first, although the signal is a little hit and miss but now it just seems to have stopped working. The battery is charged. There is a signal but no service.

I considered what I needed to do, well, finding a public phone is the obvious answer which I have done just down the road near the car park. However, this was my first stumbling block. It will not allow me to put cash in, you have to have a phone card.

Oh.

I have not got one.

I do not know if this is a specific French feature or whether it is that long since I have used a phone box that they are all like that. So, my next issue was where to get a phone card. There was something lodged in my memory, again I do not know how or why, that you get phone cards in France from a bar. And as luck would have it, we live next door to one, so that is fortunate. I, therefore, turned around and all three of us walked back down to said hostelry where I entered first full of bravado and with some confidence that this would be a piece of cake.

Wrong!

I went to the bar and I said in my best French, "Excuse me, I want a phone card."

Now, I do not know if it was my accent or the words that I was saying were incorrect but the barman just looked at me and gave a Gallic shrug.

Does that mean they do not have them or he does not understand me?

So, I repeated my request. Again, he gave me the same response, which was a little disconcerting as he is not speaking a single word in response.

Oh.

After completely ignoring me, he has wandered off to do something else and we have retreated from the bar a little embarrassed and a touch confused.

I knew they definitely did not have them in the shop below us, so I put my thinking cap on again. "I know," I shouted gleefully. "I bet they have them at the supermarket!"

This was the second stumbling block. Our village does not have a supermarket.

However, I do know that we have one in the next village about an hour's walk away. I know that they have one there as we had used it for our shopping before Mr C returned to the UK. Finding the village was not hard as it was signposted and although we were all a little hot and bothered when we got there, we made it in one piece. We located the supermarket 'Casino', not to be confused with a place of gambling as a friend of ours did and entered into the establishment with a great deal of relief. We did some shopping and although we did not see any sign of a phone card, I was confident that the process was to ask at the till and one would be produced.

Wrong!

Again, I asked the question in my best French and again got the same response, although it has to be said that I did get a smile along with the shrug this time from the young lady behind the till.

I was a little exasperated by now. I did not know if they did not understand me or were being like a Frenchman I had seen in a Pink Panther film where Peter Sellers asks the man whether his dog bites and the man says it does not, whereupon the dog bites Peter and the man says , "Well, it's not my dog."

Unfortunately, I do not know how to say "Please, can you tell me where to get a phone card?" And to be honest I have found that once I have attempted to say something twice and people looked at me like I was a complete idiot, I felt like one and any rational thought goes out of my head. So we collected our shopping and went.

It has to be said that by now I was running out of ideas and the girls asking, "What are we going to do now, Mum?" was not helping my thought process until all of a sudden, the mist cleared and I said, "Ah, ha!"

The girls looked at me hesitantly and a little warily, "I bet they have one in that Tabac we passed earlier." I informed them positively and low and behold I was correct.

Once we had got the precious phone card, we made our way home.

Stumbling block three! We are at a different part of the village than where we entered it and I do not know how to get back the way we came but I am confidently leading them out towards home, purposefully predicting that this indeed is the way to the apartment.

Wrong!

It has taken us an hour and a half to finally get back to the apartment, by which time our caramel ice cream is now a milky drink and the only person we have seen the whole time was a very happy man driving a ride on lawnmower.

Well, at least we have got the phone card and apart from the German man banging on the window of the telephone box, complaining and laughing that it was just his luck to get into a queue behind three vivacious women. I finally contacted Mr C and he told me that the phone company had turned my phone off because it had been used more frequently than normal. When Mr C told them quite indignantly that I was a woman alone in France with two children and they had removed my only means of communication without my even knowing, they helpfully said that they had sent me a text to say it was switched off! No comment!!!

Friday, 10 November
Early Evening

We have got real neighbours.

We have decided to come to the apartment for a long weekend. We have not been since the end of the summer and it seems ages since we have been here.

On entering the foyer and turning on the light, all seemed to be as we left it, plastic ivy in the troughs in front of the mirror, sand covering the doormat and spider's webs gathering momentum in the corners. Yes, everything seemed to be normal, that is until we started to mount the stairs and negotiate the steep curve incline because there at the top of the treads was something unusual.

Now, I do not know why I do this but I have a habit that when I see something, I do not recognise, is slightly scary, out of place or just plain odd I develop a strange gait. My legs bend, my bottom is thrust out behind me, my shoulders go back with my neck and chin jutted out before me, I tilt my head to one side as if listening intently with my eyes open wide and my mouth shaped in an O. Then I start to walk slowly with my legs still crooked as if I am creeping up on someone. I suppose if I was to analyse what this stance resembled, I should say a cross between a startled deer and Groucho Marx, the same behaviour that I displayed in the Maison de Maitre in Bothoa, so at least I am consistent.

Thus, I ascended the remaining steps and at the summit, on the tiny landing between the two apartments was a cage.

"Ooooo, look!" I exclaimed, semi-circling the enclosure. "There's some animals in here."

"Yes," replied a matter of fact, Mr C, he obviously did not find the experience as much as an adventure as I did.

At that point, the door opened to the adjacent apartment belonging to the formidable Madame de Bonvillier and a nice young man appeared. The appearance of this apparition and the existence of the cage instantly made us realise that Madame must have rented the apartment out long term and not just for the usual weekly summer periods.

"*Bonjour,*" we greeted in unison.

The new tenant looked at us worriedly and replied, "They are not mice. They are not rats. They are squirrels."

Now two things came to mind at this point. He must be quite scared of us, of our reaction to the said rodents because he did not say "*Bonjour or Bonsoir.*" French people old and young are very formal and polite and this politeness is more prevalent in the younger generation. Children, teenagers and young adults have a great respect for their elders and as we were clearly of an older generation, this omission of greeting was quite evident, so I think he was a little worried about how we would react. Secondly, they did not look like squirrels to me.

"Chinchillas," I responded helpfully.

"They are not rats," he repeated.

"No Chinchillas," I stated again.

He looked at me with that air of well, I have no idea what she is saying to me but she does not seem to have a problem with them.

"They are okay?" he enquired.

"Yes, yes, fine," I returned.

"Oh, okay, *Bonsoiré,*" he stated and entered his apartment and closed the door.

It turns out that Chinchilla in French is *Le Chinchilla.* Well, that was what I was saying but without the *le.* It also appears that within the rodent family that Chinchillas are part of, so are squirrels. Shows how much I know, perhaps, it was my superior 'Dr Dolittle' attitude and my incomprehensible pronunciation that confused him.

Saturday, 11 November

Just what do I have to do?

We have just been to the restaurant next door. You know giving the local establishments our support instead of going into Morlaix or Roscoff and spending our holiday money there, do they appreciate that? No, they do not!

I feel that I have prostituted myself again with this language, this tongue, which seems to laugh up its sleeve at all my efforts while offering me up as a sacrifice on the altar of my inadequacies.

Enough of that. I do not really speak like that but I am just trying to make a point. I can speak and write like that if I so choose. I just choose not to, more from a nod to my northern roots than from any other consideration. I actually think I am quite an intelligent person, if I was to analyse myself, not that

I have a 'chip on my shoulder', of course hailing from Lancashire. I have spent nearly 50 years attaining a level of interaction with people from all walks of life, from family, adults and children to colleagues, chauvinistic gits and arrogant tossers! I have written reports, tenders, documents etc. for institutions, businesses, educationalists and government bodies. I have even taught oral and written communication skills to pubescent teenagers, for God's sake. But can I speak to that man next door?

No, I cannot!

I thought long and hard about this problem, too long probably and decided that the best policy was to practice. If I knew what I wanted to say and I could say it, then that should work. I have to admit that in my innocent eagerness to be understood by 'him', I had not taken into consideration any outside influences, things like I would get nervous, blush from the roots of my hair to the tip of my toes or that people in the restaurant would stare at me and make me more self-conscious. No, because after all, I AM an intelligent person, I know I am!

So, I practiced before I went in. I practiced while I studied the menu, which I already know inside out because I have been in there that many times, all with the same outcome I have to admit and I practiced as I saw Jean walk from behind the bar in the meet and greet area.

As Jean approached the table, I thought to myself, *I can do this, I will not be beaten. I AM an intelligent person.*

"Bonsoir, Madame, Monsieur."

Now that is another thing!

Bonsoir meaning 'good evening'. If we had spoken first and said *Bonsior*, he would have said *Bonjour 'good day'* and

37

we if we had said *Bonjour* first, he would have said *Bonsoir*. I think he is just flipping awkward!

"*Bonsoir*," we responded in unison in our best French.

"*Vous avez choisi?*" *You have chosen.*

At which point we both replied, again in unison, "Qui," and Mr C nods his head in my direction for me to tell Jean what I have chosen off the menu.

It does not seem to have any bearing on the process that every time I have been in the restaurant, I have ordered the same thing. Not because I do not like anything else on the menu but partly because it is the only salad available (for some strange reason I seem to lose my appetite the minute I step over the doorstep, well, the outside eating area) and partly because it has become some kind of point of order, battle stance, a war even, that Jean will know what I want.

So I asked for a Salmon Salad, same as I always have, "*Salade du Saumon*" in my best French accent that I know is correct because I have practiced.

"Pardon?" came the blank-faced response.

I do not know if at this point there is something in my body language that alerts Jean to my chagrin, my complete disappointment in myself. I think there must be. It may be the slow exhaling of breath, reminiscent of a balloon with a slow puncture that gives me away or the fact that this little 'farce' has been played out at every opportunity of my entering this restaurant. I do not know but something does.

"*Salade du Saumon, s'il vous plait,*" I hopefully replied.

"*Pardon?*"

Oh, for God sake. So, I resort to the universal language of an idiot abroad and point at the menu while smiling apologetically for my stupidity.

Six months now and he still looks at me like I am speaking Russian.

Orange Hair and Lollipops

Friday, 16 March

Early Evening

That was different.

Primel Tregastel in March.

When we bought the apartment, we took out insurance cover for the contents of the flat. At the time of applying, it did make me smile when asked if we had any expensive jewellery or antiques? The answer was obviously, no, but as a stipulation of the policy we had to visit the apartment at least once a month, every month. It is fair to say we have not achieved that but have visited mainly in the summer, end of autumn and between Christmas and New Year, but never in the dead of winter until now.

We arrived at the apartment at about 19.30 (notice how French I am becoming using the 24-hour clock) in pitch black with the wind howling through the air and the sea crashing onto the shore, as we got out of the car the noise was astonishing. We rushed to the foyer battling against the elements and bursting in like a couple of giggling school children, which seems to be becoming a bit of a theme. As we carried on running to the turn in the stairs, we were met by the shape of a man hanging from the ceiling. Amazingly we did not jump out of our skin and run back through the door screaming. We are, after all, getting quite good at this French lark. Instead of being frightened, I was intrigued and soon came to realise, after intense staring and squinting, it was a wet suit belonging to our neighbour Francois, which he had hung up to dry, of course.

On arrival in the apartment, we put on all the lights and heaters and then decided we would have a cup of coffee before going for the 'all humiliation' meal in the restaurant next door. As Mr C plugged the kettle in, the electricity went off.

Oh.

Now was a good time to use our newly bought torch, purchased for such an occasion, that is if we could find it in the dark. Torch located, Mr C proceeded to look at the lounge light socket with suspicion and press the switch up and down with precision and regularity. I, in turn, looked at him a little confused.

"What are you doing?" I enquired, maybe a little sarcastically.

"What does it look like?" came the response.

"Well, it looks like you just keep switching the light off and on," I replied a little warily because I had noticed his tone.

"Yes."

"Oh."

"Why?" I ventured quietly.

"Because the electricity has gone off," was the rather testy reply.

Now, I have noticed this with Mr C, when he says one thing, he often means something else but I have to say on this occasion I just thought he was stating the flipping obvious. And why was he doing it? When in the UK, he would have immediately gone to the fuse box? I think, on reflection, it was because we were in France. He felt at that time that they did something different here, which sometimes is definitely the case, but not now.

"Do you think we should find the fuse box?" I gently suggested.

"I don't know where it is," replied Mr Testy.

"I know, I've got an idea. Why don't we go next door to the restaurant, have something to eat and drink and then go to the bar and get pissed and worry about the electricity in the morning when it's not dark?" I enquired questioningly.

A funny thing happened; I cannot be completely sure as we were shrouded in torch light at the time but it seemed as though Mr C was looking at me as though I was someone who had gone completely stark raving mad. This is strange in itself as usually the suggestion of the consumption of any kind of alcohol is accepted with enthusiasm.

"If you think I am going to wake up tomorrow morning with you with a hangover and you can't have a cup of coffee, you have got another think coming," he stated incredulously.

Fair point.

"What are we going to do then?" I ventured.

"We are going to ask Francois where the fuse box is," he replied in a superior tone which inferred, "Idiot, why didn't you think of that?"

Francois is around 25 years of age and shared the next-door apartment with his girlfriend and the famous squirrels out on the landing. They were renting the flat for six months during the closed season and luckily for us, he spoke better English than our French.

Mr C knocked on the door and we awaited the arrival of Francois. He did not take long to answer and opened the door enquiringly. Mr C explained that we had no electricity while I fought hard not to giggle at the plaid old man slippers Francois was wearing.

It appears that the week previously, the sea had ventured up the road and flooded into the fuse box for the two apartments and the shop downstairs. On enquiry, Francois did know where the fuse box was and so started a sequence that was eerily like a French farce.

"You need a handle," explained our neighbour.

"A handle?" questioned Mr C.

"A handle," stated Francois.

"A handle," commented Mr C.

"A handle," repeated Francois.

"We need a handle?" Mr C confirmed to me.

"Oh, we need a handle," I concurred encouragingly.

"You have a handle?" enquired Francois.

"We have a handle?" I asked Mr C.

"We have a handle" Agreed Mr C.

"We have a handle," I informed Francois, who smiled and said *Au revoir* and retired back to his apartment.

"Have we got a handle then?" I asked Mr C.

"How the bloody hell do I know!"

For goodness sake!

We sheepishly returned to Francois at his apartment and as he opened the door for the second time. We both said in unison, "We haven't got a handle."

This statement from us did not seem to faze Francois and it transpired he knew someone who did indeed have a handle, a gentleman across the road, who was renovating a *longere*. Mr C went with Francois to visit said gentleman to borrow his handle while I waited at the front door for their return with the elusive implement. As an aside, it transpires that Mr C had a bit of a fright when meeting the owner of the handle as he was in the midst of removing plaster from the walls and looked uncannily like a ghost, that or Ronald McDonald.

When Mr C and Francois returned, they were carrying a screwdriver.

Ahhh.

This unfortunately was not the end of the electricity farce. Firstly, the fuse box had to be located and the fuses returned to their operating positions. The fuse boxes for the two apartments and the shop downstairs Francois informed us were to be found in a wooden cabinet behind the aforesaid *magasin* outside in the stormy, cold, windy and very dark garden. Luckily, we had the very useful torch and Francois was being very helpful by carrying a lit red candle in a jar, that was not faring too well in the billowy conditions.

Yay, we located the cabinet and the handle/screwdriver/*tournevis* was utilised to open the door. Inside the cabinet were six fuse boxes, three on the top row and three on the bottom row.

Mr C then calmly enquired of me, "Which one is it?"

I seem to be having a great many of these 'slow motion' episodes in France, where time seems to stand still, where I cudgel my brain to endeavour to produce the correct response to the question posed to me. It has to be said that upon this occasion there was some incredulity in my receipt of this request, verging on hostile as I had never before in my life viewed this receptacle holding six devices for three homes and how the hell was I supposed to know?

I flippantly replied, "Top middle."

This response appeared to satisfy Mr C and I do not know why but he seemed to be oblivious to the note of sarcasm in my voice and on hearing it he pressed the corresponding lever down.

At which point Francois declared, "My girlfriend is now in the dark."

Later

I decided tonight after our foray into household maintenance, which appears to have given me some sort of false confidence and following my total defeat in the restaurant next door last time that I am not going to be beaten. I thought I am NOT going to point at the menu when he says pardon in his 'oh, it is such a shame for her' manner. I am going to say it in French again and again until he understands me. I am NOT going to sit there looking like an imbecile.

Before we went to the restaurant, I did my usual practising and I really thought that this time I was word perfect and I was sooooooo ready for him.

We went through the usual formalities, the *Bonjour* versus *Bonsoir* fiasco, had we chosen etc. and so in my best French I asked for *Salade du Saumon* as usual, accompanied by the polite please and thank you.

He just stood there, looked at me and said straight-faced, "*Pardon?*"

So resolutely and confidently I repeated my request, "*Salade du Saumon,*" without reference to the menu and in my best clear French.

He looked at me blankly and said again, "*Pardon?*"

I looked at him with what I should imagine by this time was blatant hostility in my eyes but I was NOT about to be beaten, so I smiled sweetly and I repeated my request, "*Salade du Saumon, s'il vous plait.*"

"*Pardon?*"

I was, I have to admit, by this point getting a little defeated, but I was not going to give in, so I calmly asked for it again in my best French and still elicited the same response.

At this juncture I am sad to say I crumbled like the imbecile and total wimp that I obviously am. I looked at Mr C in my chagrin and said in English under my breath, "I can't do this anymore."

It was strange. It was as if time stood still, like in one of those slow-motion excerpts from a film, all external sound was extinguished and the only focus in that restaurant was my face showing the complete and utter defeat I felt and the visage of Jean demonstrating the superior attitude he so clearly felt. He looked directly at me and he said in perfect French, the language of his birth, "Ha, I understood you the first time."

Bastard!

Saturday, 21 May

We have had visitors arrive yesterday; I think this will become a regular occurrence now that we have a holiday home. The visitors are Phil and Jim, both of whom Mr C and

I have worked with for some years. When I say they arrived yesterday, we all actually arrived together, flying into Dinard Airport. We came in from East Midlands and a little later they arrived from Stansted.

When I say 'Airport', it is really more like a big shed in a field. I think it has four flights in and then out each day from Stansted, East Midlands, Jersey and Guernsey.

It is an experience.

It is a bit like a comedy sketch with a limited number of cast members with all the airport personnel taking on the roles of different characters during the process. If you hire a car, a very nice lady performs the booking in etc. She then scoots across the hall to become the flight check in assistant, who then miraculously appears at the doors to the runway to check your passport for what seems to be the 900th time.

When entering the country, you land on what must be the shortest runway in the world. I have been known to violently apply virtual brakes on many occasions. You, then taxi into an area which could only be described as a yard as you wait for the man who has helped the plane park, retrieve and place his ladders at the back door to enable disembarkation from both ends on the plane. Just try to avoid arriving on a French bank holiday as the 'B' squad are in operation and it is not uncommon for the substitute ladder man to nearly knock the plane over with his excess zealous placement of said, "*escalier.*" You also need to hope that it is not raining when you disembark as not only do you get wet through walking to the arrivals lounge (slight exaggeration it is just a big room), but the luggage conveyor belt which starts just outside the door and continues for about 12 feet inside is known to react badly to adverse weather conditions and will cease working completely. This results in all the passengers standing just inside the arrivals lounge while the ladder man and his colleague literally throw the suitcases at the waiting people.

It takes about two hours to drive from the airport to the apartment and we decided instead of going immediately to the restaurant next door and then onto the bar, we would spend the first night in Morlaix and go to the Grand Café de la Terrasse for a meal. The restaurant was established in 1872 and is very grand in décor, although the toilets in the back passage leave a lot to be desired especially if you have to use the traditional French one. The café is very famous and was the starting point in Morlaix for the Tour de France. It had apparently been occupied by the Germans in the Second World War, who had caused some damage but the restaurant has been restored to its former glory.

Mr C, Jemima and myself had been for meal there once before and had caused a bit of a stir, so I was hoping they did not remember us! We had been in at lunchtime on the previous occasion and the patroness had come over to take our order and we had all decided to have one of the enormous salads they serve for our '*repas*'. You would have thought we had just walked in and murdered the occupants! She looked at us at first with utter disbelief, which quickly turned to disgust and then smoothly changed into anger. She was that angry that she called one of her waiters over and showed them our request written on her order book, while vigorously stabbing the page with her finger. They then both began to look at us all with clear hostility and proceed to serve us without any other expression other than distain on their faces, while practically throwing our salads and drinks at us. I could not quite believe it and between the fit of giggles and spillage avoidance tactics we had to employ, we realised that we had committed a cardinal sin, we had not had three courses for lunch. Not only that but the salads we ordered, which were huge, were a starter not a main course. How silly of us.

When we arrived last night, we realised that we should be okay with our choices as most French people have a 'snack' in the evening and this appeared to be the case as the patroness was all smiles when taking our order and there was none of the grimacing and gesticulating to other members of staff like the last visit. The meal went well and it was only at the last hurdle of the dessert that we displayed our total ignorance. Mr C and I do not have a sweet tooth so we were not having a dessert but both Phil and Jim wanted one and poured over the menu trying to decide what to choose. One choice contained '*miel*', did we know what that was? Well, yes, we did.

On a previous visit we had taken Gaston at the bar, some bottles of English beer as a present, coal to Newcastle I suppose. One of the bottles contained honey and we tried to explain to Gaston what honey was. We just did not know the word so we resorted to actions and both stood at the bar like complete idiots buzzing and flapping our arms around trying to imitate a bee. Gaston regarded us in confusion. We just continued to buzz and flap madly until the only other customer, who was seated at the other end of the bar called Gaston over and said something we did not hear and the confusion miraculously lifted from Gaston's face to be replaced by a grin. He walked back to us and said, "Oh, Buzz! *C'est miel.*" We had been buzzing in the wrong accent.

They decided after much discussion that they would have the dessert with the honey, even though cheese and honey sounded a little strange but you know when in France. I wish

I had a camera to capture the look on their faces when their pudding arrived. It was yogurt with honey, Fromage Frais!

Sunday, 22 May

It is very strange this foreign language thing, it is quite a conundrum that exercises my mind a little too much for a woman of my age but I find really interesting, sad I know. There appears to be several types of French people when it comes to speaking their language, about five kinds. A generalisation I realise but not far wrong and they are split between the old and the young. There is the older person like Madame de Bonvillier, who speaks to you in French at the speed of a runaway locomotive with no consideration or even thought that you do not understand or that you can respond. They do not care whether you reply or not, they have told you what they want to and that is that. There are then the older people who just cannot grasp why you would be in their country and cannot understand or speak their language. You are in France, for goodness' sake! They tend to look at you with sheer disgust when you try to reply to a question and invariably walk away mumbling and waving their arms at you dismissively.

The other set of older people are those that think because you are foreign, they can speak about you within your earshot and you will not have a clue what they are saying or indeed that they are speaking about you. The lady with the orange hair is an example of this. We had come to realise by careful people watching that there are two distinct sections to the beach. If you are a local, you sit on the smaller part to the left of the walkway on the fluffy sand and if you are a tourist you sit on the much larger side to the right with the flat sand. It is quite comical to watch this tableau in process and often culminates in people sitting so close that you could eat each other's sandwiches on the local side and masses of space on the other. The lady with the orange hair obviously sits on the local side and one of her main objectives it appears is to hand out boiled sweet lollipops to the local children while gossiping with her comrades. On one occasion we were the topic of conversation. It appears I am the lady with the two young girls and the debate was whether I am English or American. She could not tell (it is the northern accent; it throws them as I do not and never have spoken like the queen). This discussion was had with their complete knowledge that I had no idea what they were saying.

The younger people on the other hand seem to be split into two types, both kinds are more tolerant of bad French and bumbling English women. I think it is probably because at school they have had to learn a foreign language, whereas the older members did not. The first section may not speak English but do know a few words and try and work with you to come to a mutual understanding using which terms they know and general gesticulating and laughter along the way. The second set of younger people were in the bar last night.

We decided that we would stay around the apartment and go to the restaurant next door and then stroll along into the bar. Phil had actually frequented both establishments on a previous excursion when he visited the apartment earlier in the year with Mr C and two friends for a 'boys weekend'. I do not know much of what went off, apparently, what happens in Primel stays in Primel, yeah! Primel is just so riotous off-season. Although I do know that Phil did attract a female admirer, but I think generally they did a lot of drinking and eating! What I do know is that they went into the bar next door at about 15.00 in the afternoon and systematically drank their way through the different types of beers until 17.00 when they decided they would go back up to the apartment for a nap before a big Saturday night in downtown Primel Tregastel. Mr C asked Gaston for the bill at that point to which Gaston asked whether they would be returning to the bar later in the evening, to which Mr C concurred, so Gaston said to pay when they went back later. I do not think that would happen in All Bar One. After their nap they went next door to the restaurant, ate crepes and drank copious amounts of Cider and then returned to the bar at around 22.00. They remained drinking in there until 3.00 on the Sunday morning, at which point they decided that enough was enough and after 12 hours asked for the drinks bill, it was 48 euros! Apparently, there is one price if Gaston likes you and another if he does not, thank goodness he likes us.

We thought we would follow the same pattern last night, go to the creperie and then retire to the bar for drinks. This is where we met the fifth type, the younger person who just wants to speak English no matter what. We met Manu who is a local but had lived in Plymouth for 16 years with his family as a farmer but had returned to France when things went pear shaped with mad cow disease. We also came across a young surfer who is visiting his grandmother in the village. Manu's English is excellent and he held court, insisting on buying us drinks every two minutes while surfer dude just wanted to speak as much English as possible on any subject that he could think of. What ensued were numerous farcical conversations with the two French people determined to speak English and us four determined to speak French. I think that there must have been lots of points lost in translation. Not all of us enjoyed this distraction, Jim was a little bit sullen at first as I think he wanted it just to be the four of us but after a few drinks he seemed to come around to the idea. The evening ended, well, morning really, with a very tried surfer who had to get up again in two hours if he wanted to catch the best waves, a very small bar bill and four distinctly inebriated English people desperately trying to dissuade Manu from taking them to an all-night lap dancing venue in Morlaix.

Thursday, 3 August

I should have told her, she just did what I always do, made assumptions.

Jessie had decided to visit the apartment on her own. She is not known for her travel experience but good for her, she was going to give it a go. She was to fly into Brest Airport, get a taxi to the train station, get on a train to Morlaix and then a taxi here, quite an adventure for someone who had never been to France on her own before or anywhere else abroad for that matter.

I had been on tenterhooks all day, although we had agreed to keep in touch by text. Luckily, I had sorted out my mobile with the phone company. I had received a few encouraging missives, she was at the airport, she had landed in Brest. She was at the train station and bought the ticket, hooray!

That is when it all went awry!

I suppose it is a stupid thing to say the trains, stations and the ticket buying process is different in France than at home. I imagine most people would accept that. They have double decker trains for one thing so that is different but no. Jessie is obviously her mother's daughter and assumed that everything was the same in both countries, even though you cannot buy a 'return' ticket in France but this would not have been a consideration anyway as she was only going one way. So, she purchased her '*billet*' for Morlaix as instructed.

What I failed to include in these, what I thought, detailed guidelines, was to make note of the seat number allocated and make sure you sit there. Unfortunately, as this specific instruction was omitted, Jessie grasped her ticket in some triumph mixed with relief and boarded the train and sat down at the first available place presented, very pleased with herself. As the train approached Morlaix, Jessie vacated her seat, moved along the carriage, retrieved her luggage and stood expectantly at the door of the train to alight. The train came to a stop and Jessie awaited the opening of the carriage door. This did not happen. Jessie was not alarmed at first as she presumed the conductor had just not pressed the button or something but became a little agitated when she glanced out of the door window to see track and not a platform and further confused when the train began to move, passed through the station and onto the next station destination.

I myself was a getting a little concerned as I had not received the obligatory text message informing me that she was in a taxi heading for the apartment, however, after about 15 minutes I heard the comforting noise of my phone pinging, "Mum, will you ring me? I am in the middle of nowhere!"

I duly called. "Hello, love, where are you?" I enquired.

"I don't know," she wailed.

Not very helpful for a search party.

"Have you got off the train then?"

"Yes, but not at Morlaix. It stopped and wouldn't let me off and then set off again. I got off at the next stop." She moaned.

"What is it called?" I asked gently, making a mental reprimand that I should have told her to sit where her ticket said as only the first four carriages stopped at Morlaix.

"I don't know," she replied testily. "Something beginning with g, I can't pronounce it."

"Well, spell it for me," I responded, trying to sound soothing and in control.

"Guingamp."

"Ah, that's where Gingham comes from." I trilled, not a helpful piece of trivia at that point. "That's miles away." Again not a very comforting response.

"Well, don't worry. Just get on a train back the other way to Morlaix and follow the instructions from there." Assumptions again.

Jessie agreed that she would go and look for a timetable as the station was not manned and I would ring her back after ten minutes as she was getting low on credit.

After the agreed ten minutes, I called, "Hi, love, how did you get on?"

"Well, I found a timetable but there is not a train back for four hours," she replied slightly defeated.

"What!"

"That's what it says," she replied stroppily.

Oh.

"Are there any taxis?" I asked. At that point I was not holding out any hope but it was worth a try.

Jessie wandered outside the station and luckily, thank the lord, there was a solitary taxi.

"Right, well, tell him where you want to go and agree a price upfront," I stated confidently.

"Okay, Mum, but my battery is low, I'm going to go cos I might need it later." With which she went, and all communication ceased.

Oh, I hope not.

The next half-an-hour was pretty tense, every two minutes I kept getting up and looking out of the window in the hope that I would see her alighting from a taxi. After what seemed forever, she did just that and I went downstairs to meet her.

The taxi driver was a lovely man, thank goodness and we had a little conversation about how initially he was taking her to Tregastel as he had never heard of Primel Tregastel before and both of them had poured over his map book in the boot of his car to locate where it actually was.

All's well that ends well, I suppose and as we sat on the beach in the lovely sunshine later that afternoon, Jessie enthused, "Oh, it was all so worth it."

Well, it would be. I paid the 75 euros!

Saturday, 5 August

I hope that Jessie has not come here for a quiet few days because that is not going to happen.

The majority of people in France have their main summer holidays around four weeks in that season. The last two weeks in July and the first two weeks in August. There are of course exceptions like the wrinklies, who tend to go on holiday at the end of August but mainly those four weeks are the holidays for the French workers. Therefore, most planned activities are geared around that period, hence the *FestNoz*.

Last year I was on my own with Jemima and Daphne when the *FestNoz* took place in the bar next door. It is a pop concert, which spans over three days of the weekend. It is a little difficult to get away from joining in when you live next door and your balcony overlooks the beer garden where the stage is erected each year. You might as well be resigned to the fact that for those nights you are not going to get much sleep and just immerse yourself in the spectacle. There is a law in France apparently that says any public party type celebrations must stop by two o'clock in the morning and indeed this was the case last year. The bands had stopped playing by that time. However, that did not deter revellers tumbling, quite literally into the street whilst fire eating and playing the bongos until the not so early hours of the morning. I think there were some complaints from holidaymakers within the vicinity, who had not expected to spend their vacation in the middle of a circus crossed with Woodstock. The gendarmes duly arrived the follow morning and spoke to disgruntled tourists, made notes and passed the findings onto Gaston but as is typical in France the exact same thing happened the next night.

The music played is quite varied from very 'durgy' music which has an intro that promises a jolly tune but that swiftly turns into a lament by a tortured soul to bongo and drum playing percussionists to the star of the show. A man who has a striking resemblance to Hagrid from Harry Potter. His music is very upbeat, sung in English like a French version of a rocky Meatloaf and he has an interesting array of flashing lights and special effects to accompany his sessions.

It is all good fun and when you live next door you get a free disco in your whole apartment three nights running.

Jessie, when she finally arrived and settled in, assessed the situation immediately. She realised that Jemima and I had been alone for two weeks and things between mother and 16-year-old daughter were getting a little strained. She decided, therefore, that to give us both a bit of space she would take Jemima next door to the bar for part of the first night festivities. It appears she had become super confident in her abilities in a foreign country now she was a seasoned lone traveller and the prospect did not faze her. So, off they went to join the throng of young and old enthusiasts in the bar next door. I remained where I was with my red wine and listened to exactly what they listened to but without being crushed to death in the process but obviously that is all part of the *FestNoz* experience.

A couple of hours later they arrived back in the apartment with very contrasting looks on their faces. Jemima looked a bit annoyed and flounced off to get into her night clothes ready for the home disco whilst Jessie did her best to hide her bubbling laughter. It appears that whilst being part of the throng, Jemima was trying to act cool, aloof and grown up whilst sipping her Smirnoff Ice (totally different view in France on underage drinking) when an unfortunate incident occurred. A nice older French teenager had been watching Jemima closely from across the booth and was making regular unusual gestures at her which neither Jemima or Jessie could understand, so both decided to ignore her. Eventually, the young French lady decided she had to resort to more direct methods and walked across to Jemima, placed both hands on the waistband of Jemima's jeans and pulled them and it has to be said Jemima off the floor and then smiled knowingly and walked casually away. It appears that fashion victim Jemima's underwear being displayed prominently way above her trousers was not seen as 'chic' in France and the young helper believed that Jemima had not realised that her knickers were on show to all and sundry.

An Englishman's
Home Is His Castle

Friday, 27 April

A doll and a drum and a kick up the bum.

What the hell does that mean?

There are sayings in your life that are uttered without you really understanding what you are saying or indeed what it denotes and if analysed, would definitely not mean what it says but there are others that are oh, so true, you just did not realise how spot – on they really are.

Like, 'set in their ways' or 'you don't know someone until you live with them'.

Too bloody right!

When you buy a holiday home overnight you become very popular! It goes without saying that your family come to stay with you, that was one of the main points of buying it in the first place but you get a lot of 'friends' visiting you too. The problem is, and sometimes it is not an issue, that you live your life in a certain way and they live theirs in their way and never the twain shall meet.

It may be something very simple, such as eating habits. I do not mean whether they use a knife and fork or not but how often they eat, where they partake or how they scoff their repast. We tend to have a late breakfast, skip lunch and have a hearty main meal but 'normal' people have three meals a day. This particular custom can be easily remedied with no great impact upon ourselves as we identified when James came to stay when all of a sudden he went very quiet, which was extremely out of character, he was hungry, and so we gave him food, easy.

Val and Bill on the other hand, oh, my God.

Bill is a colleague of Mr C and myself. We have known him for years. We have worked with him, drank with him, socialised with him and have gone to his hometown, staying overnight in a hotel with the specific intention to spend an enjoyable evening in his and his wife, Val's, company, which we did. It was a logical next step then to invite them for a weekend and so we did.

They have just left. I do not think we will be inviting them back.

The crux of the conundrum is that Bill and Val see themselves as seasoned French travellers, explorers, forging ways into foreign parts and after spending many a happy jaunt to gites and cottages in various parts of the country they feel they know France in depth. They have become committed Francophiles and as such have come to expect a certain pattern to their holiday.

It all started so well. We went to meet them at the airport, collected them with no setbacks and ferried them back to the apartment without a hitch. A six-hour round journey for us but a nice ride in the back of the car for them without Bill having to drive and deal with his nemesis, the French slip road, which he believes are not sign posted correctly or with enough frequency and that you had got past the turn off before you realised it was there. However, we were the hosts and as such we like to make our guests feel happy and welcome, so did not mind the extended excursion.

I suppose we all have anticipations of how someone will react in any given situation and it was no different for me when showing people the apartment for the first time. I know I am biased, obviously I love the place and I understand that the majority of people will not feel the same. However, most people have entered our overseas domain and said, "Wow" with reference to the double height lounge/mezzanine area and the wonderful sea view and even if they did not say those specific words, they have indicated their happiness of being there with us and have at least said something positive.

Nothing. Not a word.

At first, I was baffled, surely it is good manners to say something, even if the missive is negative or non-committal but no, nothing. Then I must admit I got a bit annoyed, maybe it was the six-hour car journey or that they were not treating my 'baby' with the respect it deserved but me being me, I forced the situation.

"So, does it match your expectations?" I enquired innocently.

"Well, we didn't really have any," came the dual response.

Oh.

Well, that told me! So, at that point I thought, it is going to be a long weekend, let us all go next door to the Creperie, have a nice bottle of wine, something to eat and chill. So off we went to enjoy the evening.

It has not gotten any better.

We had become great friends with Laurent the proprietor and in our own little way we cared about his livelihood. We always take our visitors in for a meal there rather than going anywhere else, consistently buy the most expensive bottle of wine and in return he continually gives us a free coffee or brandy and we always make sure that our tip covers this freebie. It is a kind of dance. We have also become very fond of him and we believe him of us. In fact, he has become a great friend. So, it was with absolute total mortification that when we entered the restaurant ready to great him warmly Bill immediately clicked his fingers and shouted, "Garcon!"

I wanted the ground to open up and it was clearly reflected by the look of repulsion in the expression on Laurent's face. We hastily and probably a bit too gushingly tried to gloss over it with over-the-top greetings, laugher and quips while ushering Bill and Val towards our reserved table at speed.

Then came the ordering of the wine and meal, please just kill me is the overriding thought in my head. Bill does not want the best bottle of wine in the restaurant. Why would he? We could have house wine, Mr C does not want house wine, he wanted a nice bottle. Well, Bill was not paying 18 euros for a bottle of red wine. Well, you are not paying for it all, just half. And so, it went on. Eventually, thank goodness, as I was losing the will to live, a compromise was reached, a cheaper bottle was ordered but not the house wine. Phew. Although Laurent did not look too happy with this change in consumption.

Do not be so hasty, we have not ordered the food yet.

"I think I will have an omelette." Trilled Val, seemingly quite at ease with the wine choosing shenanigans, it had obviously happened before.

"Good choice," I replied relived that we had moved on and as the menu was in French, assumed the air of my helpline operator persona and said, "You can have ham or mushroom."

"I think I will have the mushroom," she decided.

"Oh, I've had that. It's very nice, the mushrooms are done in a lovely sauce." I enthused.

"I don't want them in a sauce."

Oh, shit. Well, I knew the mechanics of the restaurant probably just as well as Laurent and I knew that some things were made beforehand to speed up cooking and service like the sauces for the muscles, ingredients for the crepes and the mushroom sauce which also doubled up for a dressing for the steaks served. So, trying my best, I tried to explain this to Val, at which point Bill joined the fray. "Well, I have never been in a restaurant where you can't have what you ask for."

Not if it is not on the bloody menu, I thought but replied quite reasonably, "Well, Val, can have a mushroom omelette if she wants one? But the mushrooms are in a sauce."

No, that was just not good enough and what followed was that it descended into the tit for tat jousting that had been evident in the wine choosing fiasco with myself replacing Mr C as the witness for defence. After a while, violently aware that Laurent was not going to change his way of working in this tiny, seaside Creperie, I came up with a bright idea. "Have ham!" I exclaimed.

"I don't like ham," came the reply.

I gave up, so now the waitress is here and I have let them get on with it. I have played no part in the ensuing discussion. I have just sat sipping my, in my view, substandard wine, whilst viewing the proceedings from what I was trying to portray as a neutral stance.

Val had a steak in the end without the mushroom sauce.

The rest of the meal passed without incident and Mr C and myself were a little relieved to return to the sanctity of our apartment and open a nice bottle of our own wine. He could not moan about that could he, it was free.

At this point, necessity dictates that I must explain the layout of the apartment to facilitate the understanding of what happened next. On entering through the only door, immediately facing our bedroom, a left turn takes you into the double height, lounge / dining room / kitchen with a door leading to the bathroom in the right-hand corner. At the left-hand side of the main room is a staircase, rising to two mezzanine bedrooms above.

Mr C opened the bottle and as he reached for four glasses, Bill said that they did not want a glass of wine. They were just going to go to go up to bed. I do not know if Val wants a nightcap but she was given no choice. So, Mr C has poured our two wines, handed me mine and sat down next to me on the sofa.

At this point they said their goodnights and we responded in like as they made to mount the stairs, whereupon Bill has just turned off all the lights in the flat.

I would have dearly loved to see Mr C's face but as we are here sat in total darkness, I have no idea whether his expression resembles mine. I am sat glass in hand, said glass suspended in mid-air on route to my mouth, that orifice being wide open to match my gaping eyes, rendered so through unexpected surprise and the fact that I am trying to make out landmarks in the pitch black. Almost immediately a gurgling noise began. I thought at first that it is emanating solely from me but I am wrong. Mr C is producing the exact same sound.

As if as one, we lurched from the sofa, glasses in hand, Mr C cleverly remembering the just opened bottle, made a lunge for it and both bolted for our bedroom door. Once inside, we have erupted into the supressed hysterics that were threatening to completely overtake us.

Eventually, we have stopped laughing long enough to look at each other whilst recognising the absurdity of our hiding in our own bedroom and set off in whoops again.

It is our bloody house.

Sunday, 2 June

Tonight, we have decided to go to our favourite restaurant in Rosoff.

A great many people when visiting Roscoff, drive straight through the town when they have arrived on the Brittany Ferries Plymouth/Roscoff crossing and use that landing point as the first stage in their journey to the rest of Finistère, Brittany and the other departments in France. However, Roscoff is a nice place to visit in itself. It is by the sea with a long pier that juts out into the ocean towards the beautiful Île de Batz, has some stunning stone buildings and numerous bars, shops, restaurants and a few hotels. It feels a little bit like an English seaside resort if that is possible in France. It also has a singular claim to fame, Roscoff was the traditional departure point for the Onion Johnnies. These were Breton farmers who sold their pink onions around the UK, usually riding bicycle adorned with these vegetables and a string of bulbs around their necks. They were very popular in the 1920s as they found a new market for their produce across the channel as the onions were not selling in France. And so began the archetypal image of a 'French man'.

Our favourite restaurant is Le Surcouf. They serve predominately fish which is excellent but I have to say it is a little off putting to be watched closely by the crabs and lobsters floating in the fish tank, awaiting their fate while you devour one of their pals. As usual we have had a first-rate meal followed predictably by our favourite deserts of *Mousse au Chocolat (*which for some reason always seems to be a double portion, regarded jealously by the other diners) for Mr C and *Île Flottante* for me, washed down with a very nice bottle of red.

We decided to return home along the coast road around the bay of Morlaix, however, to access that route we first have to traverse a section of dual carriageway near St Pol de Leon. As was normally the case, we seemed to be the only car on the road tonight and as we drove down the slip road to join the main thoroughfare, Mr C slowed down, looked both ways and then accelerated onto the principal highway. It was at that point it happened, out of what appeared to be thin air a man appeared waving and gesticulating.

The man is a gendarme and we have been directed to leave the road immediately, drive down a dirt track and to park in front of his colleague, who is sat in a police car in the middle of a field. I looked at Mr C as we came to a halt and pulled a face not unlike a character out of Wallace and Gromit and awaited our fate.

It did not take long. The gendarme from the middle of the road followed us on foot into the field, bent down and put his head into the car through the now open window. It was by this time turning to dusk, which seemed to add to the drama somewhat.

The police gentlemen began explaining to us why he had pulled us over. Unfortunately, he was speaking very quickly and neither Mr C, nor myself could understand a word he was saying, so Mr C said helpfully, "*Pardon, je suis anglais* (Sorry, I am English)."

To which the policeman replied with authority and of course in French, "You are in France now, so we will speak French"

To which Mr C responded candidly, "Well, that's not a problem for me." Inferring, quite correctly, that it may be a slight issue for the poor gendarme to understand the attempted French which Mr C was going to utter.

The conversation then proceeded surprisingly after his adamant speech with the policeman speaking in English with Mr C trying his best to respond in French. The officer explained to Mr C that he had not stopped at the junction with the main dual carriageway and had proceeded over the continuous white line and therefore committed a traffic offense. He then commandingly uttered a closing statement of, "In France, sir, stop means stop."

It is strange that some road signs in France are in English, for some there is no direct translation, for example, Car Park but they definitely have a word for stop, it is *arret*.

The constable then explained that Mr C would receive an on the spot fine of 90 euros and for him to get out of the car and follow the officer into the police car. At this point I did get a little panicky because I knew that in French law you had to pay the gendarme the fine there and then and if you did not have the cash about your person, they would escort you to a cash machine to access your funds. If you had none available, you would be placed in a cell until someone could pay your fine for you. Well, I do not know whether Mr C has got 90 euros. What if they put him in jail? How will I get home and get the money? I do not drive and I am stuck in the middle of a field, plus I am bursting for a wee!

Mr C obviously did have the 90 euros because after ten minutes of me craning my neck to try and ascertain what was happening in the police vehicle, he arrived back at the car and got in. He had a funny look on his face as he sat behind the driving wheel and gesticulated silently for me to just hold back with all the questions I had been firing at him simultaneously until we had left the confines of the field and had started on our journey.

Once we were on the road Mr C started to laugh softly.

"What happened then?" I enquired a little shortly as I had been made to wait to find out what had occurred in the police car.

"Well, I had to give all my details to the other policeman, who coincidently was very nice and spoke English straight away as soon as I got in the car. They were a bit like, good cop, bad cop." He grinned.

"I don't know what you are smiling for." I seethed. "I was scared stiff, I thought I was stuck in a field for the night and I really need to go to the toilet! Did you have 90 euros on you then?"

"Yes, I did." Grinned the Cheshire cat.

"I don't think it's funny." I fumed.

"Well, you don't know what else happened in the car," he responded somewhat mysteriously.

"What?" I questioned.

"When they had taken my details down on the triplicate carbon copy form and I had handed the money over, they asked me to read the document to ensure that everything was correct," he explained.

"So, what's funny about that?" I asked a little confused.

"Well," he confessed. "I didn't have my glasses with me, so I couldn't see properly, so I told them *Désolé, j'ai oublié mes lumières, ils sont dans la voiture.*"

For a second, I just sat in the darkness staring at him and then I began to laugh.

Mr C was by this time chuckling so hard. He had started to hiss and titter and was wiping a tear from his eye.

"What did they do?" I giggled.

"The bad cop opened the door and told me to get out." He snorted. "I think he thought he had got some nutcase in the car." He guffawed.

I just went off into whoops and it was quite some time before we both calmed down.

Mr C had politely informed the gendarme that he was sorry he could not read the document as he had forgotten his light fittings, they were in the car.

Sunday, 3 June

After the escapade last night, we decided it would be safer and, to be honest, less expensive to eat at home and then nip next door for a couple of drinks at the bar with Gaston.

On entering the bar, it looked to be your average off season night in Le Boujaron. There are the usual suspects sat at the bar and a young courting couple sat in one of the booths and of course Gaston behind the bar.

Our conversing with Gaston had settled into a pattern, to be honest, it seemed to be a common blueprint when chatting to French people who we classed as friends. Both sides would commence speaking in the opposite home language and then revert back to their own respective tongues when the going got tough, which in our case was usually very quickly. What ensued in these situations was a pretty disjointed discussion but by the end of it all parties seemed to have got the gist of what the subject was.

After ordering our drinks and as usual not paying for them until we decided to leave, we explained to Gaston about our exploits the previous evening. These explanations have obviously taken longer than would be expected due to the franglais aspect to the discussion but when comprehension had been achieved on both sides, Gaston enquired, "Which ones were they?"

At first, we were a little nonplussed but then the penny dropped. In France there are three police enforcement officers, *Police Nationale*, who mainly deal with matters in the large cities, *Gendarmerie Nationale*, who deal mainly with small towns and rural areas and *Compagnie Republic de la Sécurité* (CRS), who are the riot police and have gained a reputation of being somewhat violent in the control of *manifestations* (demonstrations). The police that dealt with us were the local gendarmes but to add another layer of confusion to French law enforcement, these provincial guys had their own specific town forces.

"*St Pol de Leon*," confirmed Mr C.

"Shit!" exclaimed Gaston. "If they were from Plougasnou or Morlaix, I would have gone with you to the police station and got you your money back."

Tuesday, 21 August

Just when do we start kissing?

If you were to speak to the 'man in the street' and you were to ask them what one of the main differences between the French and the English were when greeting each other, the majority would say that there is a lot of kissing that goes on in France. If you watch any film, television programme or read any book discussing the French, they always kiss when meeting or leaving. The number of kisses performed depends upon the area they live in. It could be two or even four. It is always an even number unlike the Dutch, who kiss three times. Apparently, if you kiss an odd number of times with the French, they will carry on until you reach an even number, blimey, that could go on forever.

Up until today, I would not have known as not so much as an air kiss has been directed my way by any French person. But it turns out today is the key date! Over two years after we started coming here.

Literature states that commonly the lapsed time between arriving in France and the kissing beginning is normally six months, so we must be generally repugnant or it is because we do not live here permanently that has caused this delay.

Jessie and Zach have come to visit us for the week. They are sleeping in the mezzanine bedroom, which is proving to be a challenge for all concerned when Zach is required to go to bed. He dutifully dons his pyjamas, drinks his milk and submits to being placed in bed and that is when the fun and games start! It is not really Zach's fault. He is only little and very nosey to boot. He so does not want to miss out on what is happening with his mum and his grandparents down below. It reached such a pinnacle last night that Mr C told him he would nail his feet to the floor if he got out of bed again. I think Zach believed him. But obviously this state of affairs cannot go on for one thing if anyone heard they may think we really mean it and report us. For another, Zach is not daft and he would cotton onto it very quickly that it would never happen, even though Grandad has given him evidence that indeed he did have a hammer.

We all agreed that tonight we would try a different approach to the bedtime regime and that we would get him so tired that when we played the obligatory game of 'Up' (Gin Rummy to everyone else) at the kitchen table, we would not have a fourth contestant trying to join in. So, we decided to eat out, go to the bar for an aperitif and then next door to the restaurant.

Gaston was nowhere to be seen in the bar when we partook of our usual *Kir Bretons* (different flavoured liqueur depending on your taste, mixed with cider instead of the customary white wine), which was very untypical as Gaston did not generally have a night off during the summer season. Once we had finished our beverages, which was not as leisurely as it sounds, due to the intermittent need to chase Zach up and down the street and around bar tables, we walked the small distance from the bar, past the apartment stairs and into the restaurant next door.

We have been greeted as normal by Laurent, performing his perfected front of house duties as of one whom had become accustomed to this habitual process being repeated frequently every day and not fazed by the shenanigans with Bill and Val. However, we have had to approach him at the bar rather than him approaching us due to how busy the restaurant is. Fanny, one of the waitresses, after greeting us warmly showed us to our table and as we went to be seated, we noticed that Gaston was actually in the restaurant having a meal with a young lady.

"Do you think it's his girlfriend?" I enquired of the occupants of the table generally.

"How should I know?" responded Mr C with that. I am not bothered whether it is or not and it has got nothing to do with you tone.

Jessie and I were intrigued though and we kept sneaking a glance in their direction at every available opportunity. I do not think we were that discreet though to be truthful.

The meal went as expected. The food was excellent but the ambience at our table was a little less relaxing than anticipated owing to the fact that it was necessary to curb Zach's tendency to throw food around the restaurant and escape captivity at any given time. When the meal concluded, Jessie said that she would take Zach home to the apartment, get him ready for bed and by the time we had drunk our Irish coffee and paid the bill, he would be ready to say goodnight to us and go sleepily up to slumber.

We ordered the aforesaid Irish coffee and chatted happily and with not a little relief that we could actually sit comfortably without the need for ongoing negotiation with a lively two-year-old. Our hot drink arrived swiftly at our table, delivered by the incomparable Fanny.

Some explanation is required at this point to explain the amount of alcohol myself and Mr C had imbued up until this point. We had partaken of the *Kir Bretons* in the bar and had half a bottle each of a very nice Saint Emillion red wine and we were now going to drink what appeared to be my body weight in whiskey mixed with a little coffee and cream. It could be said, not unsurprisingly that at this conjuncture I am slightly tipsy.

Just as a lovely, warm glow was enveloping me, the outstanding Fanny appeared at our table carrying two enormous brandies. I was a little confused at this point as we had not ordered them and Fanny did not normally make this kind of mistake, so I was just trying in my best drunken French to explain that they were not ours when she explained that Gaston had sent them over for us. At this statement Mr C and I turned in unison and waved at Gaston and his lady friend and said which we thought was very quietly but was in fact shouted across the restaurant "Merci" and I think (I recall with shame) I shot them both my alluring Wallace and Gromit toothy grin.

I am not a big fan of brandy, it has to be said but because I been bought it specifically by Gaston and was now being watched (probably because of my shrill drunken merci) by most of the restaurant, including Gaston and his lady friend. I have had to drink it and cannot not syphon it secretly into Mr Cs glass. I think I have managed hopefully to drink it with as much elegance as I could muster in the circumstances and did so I believe without resorting to pulling faces and grimacing at the taste.

Just as we were nearing the end of this marathon brandy drinking episode, the wonderful Fanny appeared at our table again. I think it is fair to say that at this point I was getting the suspicion that Fanny was not as efficient as she would have you believe because in her hand were two more enormous brandies, that she placed on our table. I was so tipsy at this point that it is amazing I could see the glasses of the aforesaid distilled spirit but I was not that drunk to know that we had definitely not ordered them. A grinning, not so discreet glance in the direction of Gaston confirmed that he had not ordered them either.

Looking at her with a mixture of confusion and censure for her lack of waitressing acumen, I was about to explain kindly that these were definitely not ours when she stated that these drinks were on the house and had been sent over by the 'patron'. We said our slurred 'mercis' while I was looking at Mr C pleadingly, with my eyes saying "I can't possibly drink this" with Mr Cs staring back at me with the usual "You are on your own, you are going to have to. It is rude not to." Thanks.

At that moment Gaston and his lady friend had risen to leave and were approaching our table to say *bonne soiree*. We stood up not too steadily on my part, to say goodbye and that was when it happened. Not only did Gaston kiss me goodbye but so did his lady friend. I could not quite compute what was happening. There did not seem to be any logic to me as to why we were getting these '*bisoux*'. We had known Gaston over two years and I had never met this lady before in my life. It was a mystery.

I plopped back down in my chair to try and consume the awaiting quadruple brandy whilst contemplating the kissing situation and trying to comprehend what was different tonight than any other time. I cannot do it; I cannot work it out which has now been compounded by the actions of Laurent. As we wobbled happily out of the restaurant after paying our bill, Laurent came around to the front of the counter, as we were the last customers and kissed me.

What?

Why now?

Was Laurent trying to compete with Gaston and his lady friend or had that tactile couple released a canoodling frenzy?

We left the Creperie pondering loudly between us this question and realised on ascending the stairs to the apartment that it was a full hour and a half since Jessie and Zach had left to get ready for bed. As we opened the apartment door sheepishly, we espied them both sat waiting on the sofa facing the front door, clad in their bedtime attire and with an air of worry Zach wailed, "I thought I'd lost my grandad!"

Shrimp in My Knickers, Grasshopper in My Bed

Thursday, 22 May

Well, what do you say?

A little while ago I was just chilling, sitting on the sofa, doing nothing in particular when I had a peculiar feeling around my bare feet. At first, I could not quite compute what was happening but gradually it started to dawn on me. They were getting warmer, nothing that unusual there but they were also getting wetter.

What the hell?

I looked down and there emerging from underneath the furniture was a large puddle of hot soapy water and it was getting bigger. After a moment of puzzlement came the recognition, I shrieked and told Mr C that he needed to get out of the bath immediately as his splashing around was flooding the flat.

We knew when we bought the apartment that the bathroom had seen better days and there would come a time when it needed replacing, which is all well and good in your own language but talking about closed coupled toilets in French is not one of my best talents. Since being here I have nearly inadvertently bought two fire extinguishers and a full Health and Safety review of the apartment through my totally inadequate understanding. It is not just the technical language issues but where did you find such an artisan?

We have copped out. Mr C has found an English plumber via an English website listing English tradesmen living in France.

I had tried to be fair to glean the information via a more traditional route when we first bought the apartment by asking the neighbours. Not a good outcome. Madame de Bonvillier had asked me in to look around her apartment, which was a very nice friendly thing to do but I fully understood that it was a prerequisite for me to return the favour and show her around ours. To say, she showed me around is an overstatement really, her 'harpo' as we affectionately call her did the honours, mainly pointing to what she obviously felt were areas of interest whilst wandering around not smoking the lit cigarette that constantly dangled from her mouth. She must have gone through hundreds without ever consuming any. When the tour had finished, with me uttering the expected oohs and ahhs in what I hoped where the correct places, I decided that we were on such affable terms that I could use my improving French to ask her what I believed was a sensible question.

"*Madame de Bonvillier*," I started. I have to give her full title, you understand, she is very important. "Do you know a Plumber?"

Her response is the usual shrug of the shoulders.

"A plumber," I clarified. "Do you know a plumber?"

"Eh?" came the reply from the indubitable lady.

"A plumber?" I whispered, feeling once again I had wandered into a situation I did not want to be in and knew I could not extricate myself from.

With no further ado Madame unceremoniously ushered me out of her apartment onto the corridor without a single word and with a speed unnatural in a woman of her age shut the door firmly.

I have stood here for a little longer outside our flat than I normally would, seesawing between a fit of the giggles and feeling, well, a bit indignant actually before going back in.

I have been sat here, frowning and feeling somewhat confused replaying what I had said when realisation hit. I have not asked if she knew a plumber but I have asked her does she know a fireman. She obviously thought I was not quite the ticket, either that or I had strayed into an area of her romantic dealings that she did not want to discuss.

Mr C has emailed the contact plumber for our area of France and arranged an appropriate rendezvous at the apartment. Spot on the appointed time, Ted and his wife, Prue, have arrived. Our friend, Phil, is staying with us and after a little chat and the obligatory welcome glass of red wine, Ted, Prue and I are sat at the kitchen table flicking through brochures, whilst Mr C is hovering around trying to look busy and Phil just sitting drinking his wine. Mr C is just not interested in any detail concerning DIY or interior design so it is not unusual for him not to be a part of this decision-making process. What is unusual, however, is his peculiar facial expression. Well, some people would say he has a funny face anyway. His constant glancing out of the window and quite frankly his furtive manner.

What is the matter with him?

All became clear once Ted and Prue had left. After he had confirmed that they had indeed definitely gone, he has just let out a great big whoop of laughter. Phil and I are looking at each other a little surprised and are asking in varying degrees of exasperation, he had been behaving a tad weirdly, it has to be said, what he is talking about.

"It's them." He guffawed, hitching this thumb over his left shoulder towards the window.

Oh, no, I thought, *he is getting excited about her stockings again.*

The *longere* across the road has been renovated, Ronald McDonald is the contractor employed to complete the work and has moved on and the owner has moved in to his permanent home a little while ago. He is in his 40s I would guess and as yet never even uttered a '*bonjour*' to me. Most of the time he appears to live on his own but in the summer, as per a great many homeowners in Primel, has had a stream of visitors. One such visitor is a young lady and her male companion. I cannot quite make out their relationship, my goodness, I am getting as nosey as the French but that it is no surprise about the nature of the liaison I mean. I am not very good at the amore lark. I know the French are known for their romantic intrigues but I am just rubbish at stuff like that.

Back in the UK when I was working full time and Mr C was working away, I went to a launch of some kind in London. It was at a flash Japanese hostelry which was very swishly decorated with a round bar in the middle of the room. On top of the counter were different types of sushi and the wine was flowing. A young man from Mauritius came over to me and started chatting and he did a sterling job at ignoring my failed attempts at eating sushi in a ladylike manner. You try biting though a piece of raw fish. He was very nice around 26 I should think. He was telling me about his island, the culture, the people and I was having a very nice discussion with him, even when he said that his mother and sister in Mauritius, would like to meet me and I should go, did anything untoward enter my head. It was not until several minutes later when he tried to feed me a king prawn, the end dipped in garlic sauce did realisation hit and my head span around in blind panic like a demonic spinning top. As I was desperately scanning the room, I espied Phil across the circular bar and after returning my panicked gaze with complete disgust at my earlier lack of comprehension, jerked his head with exasperation towards his side of the bar and said through gritted teeth, "Get over here!" I went over like a naughty schoolgirl while muttering, "I was only being motherly."

So, it is no surprise then that I cannot work out their relationship. What I do know is that she is a very attractive young lady, even I can see that and she causes quite a stir when she goes down to the beach. She seems to have a full wardrobe consisting solely of bathing attire as I have never seen her in the same one twice. All of these garments are extremely skimpy and I do not know if she knows the effect of these on the male population. I believe she does but that poor German boy had to lie on his front on the beach for an inordinately long-time last week.

"What are you talking about?" I enquired a little testily.

"Those two," he stated.

"Who two?" enquired Phil.

"The owner and the young woman." He grinned.

"Have you gone mad?" I enquired.

"What about them?" asked Phil ignoring my question.

"Well," whispered Mr C collaboratively. "When Ted and Prue were here, I looked out of the window and I saw them."

I thought he has lost it. Our apartment is on the second floor and so gives us a clear view into people's gardens and up and down the street. It is an ideal vantage point for viewing anything from the local nursery children in their sowesters and wellies on, snaking their way to the beach to the brightly coloured vehicles promoting the summer Circus, so, of course, he is able to see them.

"Saw them doing what?" Phil probed.

"Ha ha! That's the question," replied Mr C in triumph.

"Oh, for goodness sake," I responded in some exasperation.

"What?" asked Phil making a last-ditch attempt.

"Well," Mr C said whilst looking around the room to see if anyone else was listening. "She was sat astride him and they were having sex behind the hedge. They thought no one could see."

Well, that is not fair, why did he not signal to us or something? It is not like I wanted to see them 'In flagrante' but I did think I had missed out somehow.

Saturday, 28 June

Note to self – grandchildren can become completely obsessed by a plastic wheelbarrow to such an extent that severe trauma is displayed whenever said garden implement is removed from their grasp. It is so bad that Grace has got a wonderful range of grazes along her hip bones developed by the fact that her torso is permanently wedged between the yellow and red toy. We have had to come up with some very innovative wheelbarrow cloaking techniques to get in and out of the apartment to reduce the psychological impact on the poor child.

Daphne, Luke and Grace are with us for a week. Well, me really as Mr C returns to the UK after the weekend.

They have been here several times before. The first time was when Grace was a tiny baby and they arrived by boat at Roscoff. We had arranged to meet them in the car park so they could follow us home to the apartment. There was only one problem with this plan, unbeknown to us, there are two car parks. One a little higher up the hill than the other, we were at the top one. We got out of the car and stood on the edge of the car park, looking down the hill to the ferry which was already moored and we waited and we waited. Eventually, we were the only people left in the car park and all the cars disembarking from the boat had gone past us and out of the gate. Where the hell were they? It was beginning to get dark and a little bit eerie as we stood in an empty car park and then we heard it.

"Mummmmmmmmm?"

Most people may have been a little startled by this noise but not me. I was relieved. My children have got an uncanny knack of sounding like a cow mooing when shouting me. It was something I became quite attached to when they were little calling for me in the night. I knew that plea so well.

"It's Daphne." I trilled.

"Yes, but where is she?" Bemoaned Mr C.

We soon located her and the 35-minute convoy to the apartment pasted without incident. Well, except for the fact that we lost them again. It appears that on the journey over

Daphne had been a little queasy and it was not until they reached the smooth waters of the port that she felt more herself and realised that there was a bar. So, she downed two full pints of beer in the space of about ten minutes, consequently, she was desperate for a wee by the time we had reached Morlaix. We did manage to locate her after some effort in the dark. She was found crouched behind the car relieving herself whilst Grace slept peacefully and Luke sat waiting with a look of resignation.

Whilst they are here, we have invited Ted and Prue over for a meal at the creperie next door as a thank you and for them to meet some of the family as we have become big friends with them over the installation of the bathroom. To be honest, they are the only English people we know around here. The bathroom has been fitted, tiled and finished and very nice it looks too. Ted and Prue spent a week in the apartment removing the old suite and replacing it with the lovely shiny new one. They became very friendly with Laurent next door, setting up a type of pulley system over the balcony down to the ground floor that was utilised every day at 17.00 for their aperitif.

So, when they arrived and we had performed the introductions off we went next door to visit Laurent and had a lovely meal. There was some curiosity and a little disbelief amongst the French in the restaurant and indeed us too on the surprising penchant for muscles Grace has. Poor Luke could not get them out the shells quick enough. I think that he must have been a little hungry by the end of the meal as she had eaten the majority of his *moules*. He only managed to get the odd one in between Grace's shellfish lust, quite unusual for an 18-month-old child.

It may have been the lack of sustenance, although I think it is the sheer volume of alcohol consumed rather than the effect of it on an empty stomach that has led to the impromptu performance. It is getting quite late. Grace is fast asleep, Ted and Prue seem to have taken root, assisted by the copious amounts of red wine imbued and the writing is on the wall on how this one is going to end. We have been here so many times before. Daphne has made the wise decision that she and Luke should go on up to bed. That is the moment that Luke's Gypsy Rose Lee alter-ego emerged. He proceeded to share with us a carefully considered striptease up the open stairs and onto the mezzanine floor above, throwing each item of clothing removed around the apartment with sheer abandon culminating with his boxer shorts landing on Prue's head. I think it is safe to say we were all goods friends by this point.

It has been some time before Ted and Prue have made the decision that they really should commence the 45-minute drive home (dread to think) and I have by this point come to realise that Mr C is extremely drunk. Ted and Prue departed and we have gone to bed. I fell asleep almost immediately to be awoken some short time later by a peculiar sound. As I lay in the dark, I have become aware of two things. One, that Mr C is not in the bed beside me and two, the noise is coming from the newly installed bathroom. I just cannot make it out, the unusual sound coupled with my sleepy wine head will not translate the noise into something which I can immediately identify. After a small amount of time cudgelling my unwilling brain, I have realised that the sound is metallic, what the?

I have got out of bed and wandered through the lounge to the bathroom, where I can see that the light is on and the door is ajar, so I have opened it.

"What the bloody hell are you doing?" I hissed.

Mr C has not even jumped, even though I had evidently crept up upon him engaged in some very strange behaviour. He has just stood up from the crouching position he had adopted somewhere near the vicinity of the sink, walked nakedly past me in silence whilst handing me a dirty great big breadknife.

Monday, 21 July

A shrimp in my knickers and a grasshopper in my bed was not what I expected to be honest. I do not know if this herbivorous insect was maybe a cricket or indeed a grasshopper. I did not look too closely at its horns to determine the species. Also, I did not check if it leapt 20 times its own length when I disturbed it snuggled under the duvet. I just know it jumped nearly as far as I did!

The invasive crustacean on the other hand was a little more unusual and a slightly more public discovery. I have sunbathed on many a beach and I can honestly say that it has never happened to me before.

There are numerous occasions I am finding that I am totally un-prepared for. It is not that we live out in the wilds, it is just that it is a totally different kind of life, ignoring the language and culture, the whole environment is so unusual for a 'townie'.

A major selling point for the apartment was the proximity to the beach. A strong man on a good day could practically throw me out of our kitchen window and I would land on the sand. The beach is absolutely magnificent and when the tide is out, it goes on for what seems miles before the sea is reached. It is the kind of idyllic coastline that could be described in many a novel, clear blue sea, a sandy beach with enough shells for a good coquille hunt and rock pools dotted about for a perfect afternoon of messing around with a fishing net attached to a bamboo cane.

The shellfish in my bikini bottom was probably my own fault because I did not follow the beach etiquette.

Is there one? Oh, yes, indeed.

The beach is a huge expanse with a concrete ramp for seaweed collection tractor access about an eighth of the way in on the left. To the left-hand side of this entrance is where the locals sit, the sand is fluffier because the sea does not normally reach that level when the tide is in. This side is where the Primel citizens and holiday homeowners play volleyball in the afternoon watched by all the other natives. The remaining seven eights of the *plage* is for the tourists. This does not seem to be a fair and equitable division of the space to the casual observer but cultural and tourist considerations have to be observed at this point and you do not want to be seen as a day-tripper.

This was my mistake. I am sat on the wrong side, even though through previous experience I should be on the other side if I want to be a local. There is just so much more space this side.

The tide had earlier in the day ventured right up to the sea wall on the 'tourist' side and therefore when it retreated, the sand was flat and although to the naked eye it looked perfectly serviceable and very smooth it hid a wriggling surprise. I laid my towel down and relaxed into an afternoon of contemplation and untroubled laziness.

Wrong.

The little bugger was hiding just beneath the *sable* and with great determination and stealth squirmed across my towel and up my inside leg. This was closely followed by lots of squealing from me whilst throwing myself around the sand and shaking the intruder unceremoniously out of my pants. It is probably a good job I am up the other end and not sat with the locals because this behaviour is not going to get me accepted.

I did not make the same error twice. I always sit on the local side, even though space is limited and the staring and in-depth observation of my person is at an unnatural height – I do not want to appear as a holiday maker.

Friday, 15 August

Chip and Pin is here. Has France embraced this new technological phenomenon? Yes, indeed they have, but in typical French style whilst the rest of the world has gone for a four-digit number password, they have gone for five.

What the—?

James has been staying with us for a few days. He is a regular here and visited last time with Mike and Nic, which was a hoot. We had all met together at Birmingham Airport, so there were five of us who boarded the plane for Brest. James was in a relationship at the time but she was not joining us as he candidly informed me she would not like the apartment, bit rude. It appears the young lady is more akin to staying in five-star hotels and drinking champagne, well each to their own.

Once we were on the plane, four of us got the giggles but not James. He was the subject of our mirth. There had been lots of laughter previously to this but it was the reaction from James when he was asked to move seats from the front to the back of the aircraft to 'balance the weight' that did it.

He was so indignant.

Exclaiming with his beautiful, clipped, very British Sandhurst accent, "Well, I have never been asked to do this before, are you saying I am overweight?" made it even funnier.

We had an absolutely wonderful weekend, lots of eating, drinking and laughter culminating with an impromptu dance off on the terrace of the bar next to Eglise Sainte Melonie in Morlaix. I do not know how it was initiated. I think we had been discussing the previous evening sing along on the way home from Roscoff. Poor Mr C was the designated driver so he was completely sober, unfortunately for him, we were not. We were singing at the top of our voices to various Motown hits, thoroughly enjoying ourselves with the accompanying innovative seated dance movements whilst Mr C lamented the complete absence of any 'punk' renditions, which we completely ignored.

The first to compete was Mike, then Mr C followed swiftly by James, this was accompanied by wide ranging interest by the locals and tourists, varying from amusement to downright disgust. This did not seem to deter our combatants in the least, in fact I think it spurred them on further. Whilst the exhibition dance by James was being performed, the waitress approached our table and made a very valid observation. She noted that Mike danced with only his legs, Mr C with only his arms but James was the all-round entertainer using all the appropriate limbs at the appropriate time.

When we separated back at Birmingham Airport, it was quite emotional, we had had such a good time.

We are being a little more sedate with this visit and although there has still been a great deal of eating (James needs food constantly) and drinking, there has definitely been no more dancing. I think that is a bit of a disappointment for James because he so loves to dance. We have included a little cultural interlude, however, which has sparked some local interest. We went to visit Musee de Morlaix on our way out for our evening meal. It is more an art gallery rather than a museum. This did not go down well with Mr C as he is a bit of a philistine when it comes to 'paintings' but James seemed to enjoy it. So much so that he decided to explore the upper floor whereupon climbing the stairs turned to me. I was dawdling slightly and so he whistled. The female attendant was livid, went very red and then shouted up the stairs to him, "She is not a dog to be called to heel!" I think James did not understand this missive, either that or he chose to ignore it. I on the other hand thought it was hilarious, primarily for the fact that she thought that James and I were a couple and not me and Mr C. Ha Ha! Very Amusing.

After our cultural excursion we set off to Roscoff in search of food and that is when it happened. We got a puncture. It was so lucky that James was with us as Mr C is not the most practical of people and cars are definitely not his forte. Poor James instead of having the promised meal had to change the tyre for the spare and as the car 'limped' back to Primel, had to be content with a repas at the Creperie.

The next morning Mr C and James got up nice and early and went in search of a new tyre. Unfortunately, they were too early, assumptions again and so had to have a coffee whilst they waited for the garage to open and they could purchase a new *pneu*. Enquiry at the garage was encouraging. Yes, they could get a new tyre for the BMW, excellent. It would be available in September. We are at the moment in the middle of August, oh. We are only here for a couple more days, so that presented a slight problem until Mr C ascertained there was another garage situated at the other side of Morlaix that was dedicated to our make of car. They could indeed get us a new tyre, it would be available for fitting the day after, phew.

It was decided that Mr C would take James to the airport the following day for his flight home and then drop the car off at the garage on the way back for us to collect it in the afternoon. All appears to be going to plan, even getting a taxi to the garage has gone well. We have never booked a cab in France before. Once here we approached the counter to enquire if the car was ready and indeed it was splendid, all was left was to pay the bill.

Our bank card no longer tells us we are 'an imbecile' when we use it, which is good news, however, the chip and pin machine does not like it, no surprise there then. What to do? We were at a bit of a standstill until Mr C had a great idea and stated with great excitement, "I will leave my wife here as a deposit and go and get the cash from an ATM."

I have just spent the last half-an-hour being treated like an exhibition in a curiosity shop with a stream of assorted garage staff from mechanics to receptionists pointing and laughing at me with varying degrees of discreetness. Well, none at all actually.

Thanks, Mr C.

Sunday, 25 August

Sometimes you just do not see it coming.

We have settled in nicely to the 'summer' routine in the apartment. It has to be mentioned that this aforesaid habit favours myself more than Mr C, however, these customs have been adopted by both of us. I go to the flat in the summer for an interval of approximately six weeks, usually spanning from sometime in July to somewhere in September. Mr C returns from working in the UK to France every weekend over that period, each Friday night going back to the slog each Sunday. The only variance in the procedure is the type of transport utilised by Mr C. Today the France to UK leg was by boat through Roscoff. This meant that the departure time from the apartment back to the UK is set for around 16.00 and so at about 14.00 we decided to have a cuppa.

Just as we sat down to enjoy our beverages, there was a knock on the apartment door. This occurrence although unusual was no longer surprising as since the demise of the ownership of the next-door flat by Madame and the purchase by Laurent the main front door to the two flats was not triple bolted as instructed in the previous tenure and so callers could ascend the stairs to our door unchallenged.

We both looked at each other with that 'well, who can this be look' and Mr C opened the door a little hesitantly to reveal two French young ladies on the threshold. One evidently older than the other. They were both very well dressed, which should have given us an early indication and were both smiling, well, grinning at us actually.

Before we could utter the familiar *bonjour,* the older of the two said, "Good Afternoon." in English.

We were, it has to be said a little nonplussed at this greeting as it is a bit of an occasion to have any unannounced visitors. Let alone have them speak to us in English.

"We have come here from Morlaix. We are from the Anglo-French association," the elder of the two stated.

I do believe she made have said something else but Mr C is so excited to have this uncalled for visit. He ushered them in hindsight on their part, a little reticently into the apartment and shut the door.

We had been living in the apartment on and off for four years now and were, we knew, the only English owners in the village. There was a British man who worked for BT (how we knew this random fact I have no idea) who rented out his home to holiday makers but who never came to the house himself (again another piece of information gleaned from who knows where).

For some time now Mr C had been commenting on a regular basis about some organisation that must exist between the French and the English in the area. Morlaix, from where our visitors hailed, is the biggest town locally with a population of around 16,000, where nearly 7% of young children went to bilingual primary schools. It is therefore with well-founded evidence, Mr C believed, that this call is, if a little overdue, wholly expected.

"Take a seat, please," begged Mr C, graciously pointing in the direction of one of the pair of two-seater sofas.

Looking back, at this point, there was an enormous clue as to what was to come, if only we had taken note and assessed this at the time. It is not just the fact that they looked like two captured insects that had been pinned onto the apartment wall, above and around the radiator but the astonished silent 'o's shaped by their mouths before the spokeswoman uttered an amazed, "We don't normally get asked in."

"Would you like a drink?" questioned Mr C, quite oblivious, as was I, to the two ladies' incredulous expressions.

"No, thank you," the lead spokesperson replied faintly, failing to hide the look she flashed towards us, which was now quite obviously surprised.

"We were wondering when we would get a visit from you because we have been here four years now, you know." Mr C stated confidingly to the two very upright, slightly wary ladies seated on the opposite sofa. We on the other hand are very comfortably sat together, eagerly awaiting what our new visitors had to tell us.

The younger lady as usual did not say anything but smiled politely at us both, while the self-appointed leader looked across at us and said, "We would like to ask you some questions, if that is okay?"

"Yes, yes, of course," responded Mr C. "Fire away." As he sipped from his teacup.

I think that they had told us their names but in all the pleasantries I have not recalled them, so number one lady looked directly at us and asked, "So, what do you think about the love of God?"

Oh, here we go again. We were back to that again, the normal adopted stance from Mr C whenever faced with anything he does not want to answer or indeed recognise. He simply turned and looked into my astonished face as if to say "You are on your own here, love!"

I do think I have tried, maybe in vain, to achieve the correct balance between theological debate and the urgency to get our witnesses from Jehovah out of the door but I am not entirely sure I have.

Thanks again, Mr C.

Monday, 13 October

I hope no one speaks to me because I do not think I can trust myself to answer. That function is not normally an issue for me but just now I do not think I would give anyone a coherent, reasonable response no matter what the subject. I just cannot seem to get my brain in order. It is like it has had some sort of short circuit but it must be fine because I am walking up this road in a normal manner. People are not staring at me and looking askance like I am mad or whispering behind their hands, in fact, they are going about their everyday business and completely ignoring me.

"If you get a chest pain before you receive an appointment, ring for an ambulance immediately," she said.

Was she talking to me?

Well, she must have been as there was only me in the room with her.

But that cannot be right. I honestly thought she would say that I was being silly. I was overreacting, I was some sort of closet hypochondriac.

It was not at that point on my zombie like walk home or when I reached my destination, that I realised it, but something had to change.

In the end it's not the years in your life that count, it's the life in your years – Abraham Lincoln.

Je Le Veux

Friday, 19 January

I had never been to a French Wedding. Well, now I have.

If I was being totally correct, we have just been to a wedding in France of two English people, Ted and Pru, and not necessarily a totally French affair, although there were certain traditions that were upheld.

Traditionally, the French have two ceremonies – a civil marriage, this is the only legal way of marrying in France and a symbolic marriage, which is normally the second ceremony in a church. Ted and Prue have just opted for the former. They have lived together for years and decided to get married for a purely practical. 'Let's deal with the French inheritance laws surrounding second marriages' reason rather than sudden overwhelmingly romantic impulse.

As they live on the outskirts of Callac in the next 'department' to us, they chose *Monsieur le Maire, Felix Leyzour*, at the town hall to officiate the ceremony, it is the first ever marriage of English people in Callac.

We all congregated outside in the carpark waiting for the bride to arrive. Ted was already on the steps to the entrance of the building and waved to us when we got there. It is a bit nippy in this car park, it is January. I had no idea whatsoever how I should dress? Do they wear hats? It appears not by scanning the waiting guests, thank goodness for that as apart from looking like a washer woman, I cannot carry off head apparel. I would look even more out of place than I already do.

Prue arrived in a flurry of activity and in her own words commented on her appearance later as "58-year-old hid toilet roll up her dress and spent the day with her heaving chest underneath her chins." Her bridal gown is not the elegant ensemble she had envisaged but a frothy, frilly, corseted, ribboned affair that her French neighbours have insisted she wears for the occasion.

The ceremony itself was very quickly performed. The mother of the groom and the father of the bride did not walk them 'up the aisle' as was tradition as unfortunately those poor souls are no longer with us. French weddings do not have bridesmaids or groomsmen and neither do Ted and Prue. They have the witnesses as is the convention for the occasion. At the end of the procedures, Ted and Prue said, "*Je le veux.*" I want it, bit forward and a little rude I think, not the 'I do' we are used to.

We all filed out of the *Mairee* and back into the car park where we have retrieved our prospective cars. What followed is a drive around the town in crocodile form pipping and tooting at all and sundry as we traverse the short distance. Three circuits of said route to the *Halle Polyvalente* for *Le Vin D'honneur*. I have to say it feels a bit alien and a tad discourteous to be honking our horn at complete strangers but we are doing it, when in France and all that.

I think at this point we do feel a little bit like fish out of water. Not only because of our actions, our practically complete incomprehension of the wedding ceremony and what to expect next but also because we do not know a sole other than Ted and Prue. This has soon been remedied as Prue walked over with a couple Colin and Jane, who are in the same boat as us. We are getting on like a house on fire, which is good as it is destined to be a very long day.

After an hour or so, drinking Aperifits, Mr C on orange juice due to a long drive back to the apartment at the end of festivities, we are now driving to a small restaurant booked out totally for the wedding party and '*Repas de noces*' – Wedding Meal. This consists of five courses and five different types of wine to accompany each culinary delight. I am slightly squiffy, Mr C on the other hand decidedly not. Things have got a little 'interesting' during the main course of duck, they are practically quaking on the plate, much to the disgust of Colin when an octogenarian lady of surprisingly athletic ability climbed on the table in pursuit of a kiss from mallard hater Colin. Calm has been restored by her husband dragging her unceremoniously and not too gently from the table by her skirt.

She has now set her sights on me, not romantically I add, but in a collaborative informative way by telling me that she and her husband never have a cooked meal at home but went out to restaurants five days out of seven. She elaborated on this by informing me that it was a lot cheaper to eat *Plat de Jour* on those days than paying for the ingredients and fuel to make the meals herself, fair point and if her habitual drinking was like today, a lot safer.

We left the wedding party at least seven hours later than when we met them, but they were still going strong off then to congregate at Ted and Prue's house. I do not know if they followed the tradition of *Pot de Chambre*, apparently this receptacle is filled with mysterious contents, normally strong spirits and then presented to bride and groom in the marital bed to drink to give them strength and vigour for the wedding night and the years to come. Enough said.

Friday, 6 March

It must be the helpline thing. Perhaps when you work on a helpline, the helpfulness just oozes into your body and radiates outwards, ensuring that the observer is never in any doubt of your total goodwill and support. It has got to be that, otherwise I just cannot explain it.

Tonight, we are having one of our regular Anglo/French social events with our neighbour Laurent. He of the gastronomic enterprise next door and the co-occupier of the apartment building. These mini gatherings had become a regular occurrence over the autumn and winter months with the diminishing seasonal opening hours of the *Creperie* and the increase in cyclic sporting occasions related to the time of year, namely Rugby and Football. It had become the norm whenever one of these local derbies in the loosest terms was on, that Laurent would appear at our apartment door with television in hand. It was not that we do not have a television or that said television is not French. It just appears that it is not considered by Laurent as fit for purpose. So, the first 20 minutes of any sporting encounter entails the multiple positioning of the surrogate set, occasionally on top of ours, or stand-alone accompanied by constant fiddling and faffing with aerials, wires, shutters, furniture or anything deemed appropriate until Laurent was satisfied with the output. Which to the unbiased onlooker would look no different to the fizzy picture we achieve on ours.

These meetings would always include alcohol, of course, however, we would always begin with English beer, which we had introduced to Laurent when we had the first of these jamborees. He would invariably imbue a maximum of three bottles before moving onto wine as to exceed that amount would render him severely intoxicated. Unfortunately, usually after the three snifters, he would present to us his new entrepreneurial brainchild. I say to us but it was invariably to me alone as Mr C had the incredible knack of not being present physically, mentally or emotionally at the moment of the unveiling of such discoveries. It was the Jehovah's Witnesses all over again or it was this helpline thing, my face must just say, I am listening I am helpful.

We have been privy to quite a few of these exciting innovations previously, one of these being the kayaks. The two upstairs apartments and the downstairs establishment all share a lawn at the back of the property which is approached through an archway at the side. It is not a large lawn and because we are upstairs and had a balcony is never utilised by us and to be fair, all maintenance of the 'garden' is performed by Laurent's parents. We do, however, use one of the three parking spaces available. One is for Laurent's domain and the other is occupied by a dilapidated, unseaworthy boat, which Laurent is in the process of restoring; although, I have never seen any evidence of this activity taking place. The kayak enterprise is going to require access to this area as Laurent explained when he presented us with his vision. "You know, Francois, my friend, who owns the *Pizzeria in Terenez*?" he began.

"Erm, yes," I responded a little nervously. I have never physically met this man but I feel I know him very well and wondered if indeed this was a loaded question as on a previous occasion one of Laurent's bright ideas was for us to buy said Pizzeria. I do not clearly remember how we avoided becoming owners of a beachside catering establishment, but we did.

"Well, he hires out Kayaks," he stated.

"Oh," was my response, which may not have been satisfactory but apart from the fact that I am relieved that there was no animosity towards us in regard to the missed restaurant adventure, it seemed a little random to be discussing kayaks.

"Yes," he continued. "He can get them for me and I can hire them out here."

"Oh." My answers were becoming a little repetitive I have to say but I was trying to figure out what was actually going on, not helped by my large intake of red wine.

"Yes," he repeated. It was obvious that he expected a different response other than oh and would continue to keep repeating his yes until I give the correct reply. Mr C was absolutely no help whatsoever.

Mustering up my total non-knowledge of all things, kayak I said, "So, how many would you need?" I did not really need to know the answer and to be honest I was not all that interested but I was becoming a little concerned that the 'yes' and 'oh' conversation would go on forever and I wanted another glass of wine.

"400, so I will have to use the lawn," he replied triumphantly.

"400!" I responded. May be a little screechy, unconcerned about the lawn usage but more than a little astounded as to where he would get this stampede of kayak loving punters from, perhaps my helpline halo had slipped slightly.

There was no more discussion on this entrepreneurial exercise that evening, perhaps my face had reflected my inner feelings around numbers and it was only when reflecting later that we were intended to be the bankroll for this sailing adventure that the penny dropped and my astonishment had caused him to reconsider.

It seemed that we are regarded by Laurent as needing some innovative enterprise to spend all that money, we so obviously have sloshing around. Culturally, I suppose we could not blame him thinking thus as the French seldom own houses, predominantly renting, never mind have a second home in a foreign country. I think he has finally realised we are just normal people with normal salaries after the Night Club affair. It took all my wit and cunning to convince him that we were not the French equivalent of Peter Stringfellow and we did not want to buy the hotel that was for sale in Le Diben, the next village and turn it into the nightclub he so desired to run. It was not the unuttered fact by me that the total population of Primel Tregastel and Le Diben probably did not exceed a thousand, let alone many of whom were octogenarian. Or the point silently considered that a swimming pool available for a load of drunken people was not the best thought out facility, although he was very keen on it but that we just did not have that kind of money. The realisation seemed to dawn and from then on there was a definite change in tactics on his part but no diminishing of the startling ideas presented to us from him.

His next approach came out of nowhere and as it was from a totally different stance and subject, took us completely unawares. We had been in the restaurant, had a lovely bottle of wine, Irish coffees and had been sent the now obligatory brandy and were feeling well, pretty mellow, when we approached the counter to pay for the meal. During the normal, did you like it tipping etc. Laurent said nonchalantly, "Do you know what Meduses are?"

Well, as was the normal activity between myself and Mr C when presented with a French word we did not understand, we both took on the look of a startled rabbit while looking at each other with questioning and no little longing that the other knew what the hell it meant. Tonight, it was obvious that we did not know, so Laurent repeated the word just to make sure "Meduses."

No, nothing, but in the back of my mind all I was seeing was the woman with all the snakes on her head in Greek Mythology but could not think why. Mr C shrugged his shoulders and looked at me. No, I did not know either, so the usual method ensued where we tried to arrive at the meaning by a process of elimination. Although it did not appear to be going to well, it may be the amount of alcohol involved. We finally realised that it was some sort of creature that he was asking us about and after us going through all the French animal names we knew, cows and sheep, which were no help whatsoever, he gave us a visual clue, and started waving his arms about on his head.

"Jellyfish," I shouted triumphantly, may be a little too loudly.

"Yes," he confirmed. Why was he talking to us about jellyfish? All would become clear. "Are they protected species in your country?" he enquired innocently.

"I don't think so," I replied partly concerned that I could not give him the answer.

"They are in this country," he stated.

"Oh," I responded, not for the first time when dealing with Laurent in total bewilderment but knowing deep down that it was coming, the helpful person was required.

"Could you breed them for us?" he enquired while proceeding to explain that as they were a protected species in France you had to get a special licence to breed them here and he did not have one.

There were many questions running around my head at this point and it was just not right. It is not cricket. I was at an unfair disadvantage. I had been eating and drinking and was not necessarily at my dynamic best, so the first question that came spluttering out of my mouth was, "Why do you want to breed them?"

That it seemed for Laurent to be the correct response and he went into great lengths to explain what he has planned. It appears that Laurent has become reacquainted with an old friend from his university days, Romaine, who is indeed the aforementioned Marine Biologist and together they have hatched a plan, no pun intended, to produce large see-through tubes filled with water, containing an up lighter and jellyfish floating around in this environment. The tubes are to be placed in the restaurant to give the diners an unexpected ambience.

In my slightly alcoholically fuddled brain, I was trying to understand the logistics of our part in the affair. The fact that I was actually considering our function will help you understand why I believe my need for being helpful is a core part of my soul. Notwithstanding, the fact that I have no idea what you keep jellyfish in water, obviously. Do you put table salt in it or do we have to go off to Scarborough to pillage the ocean? What do they eat? Do you clean them out like goldfish? What about the logistics of the whole piece? How do you get a grown jellyfish back to France? This was a lot to be thinking about but in reality, only took a couple of seconds to filter through, whilst all the time being watched by a highly amused Mr C. Again, absolutely no help whatsoever but then a very logical question entered my head, which I voiced immediately, "How many Jellyfish?" Like I was really considering it.

"About a thousand," came the reply.

Needless to say, I managed to extract us from any obligation to breed Jellyfish in the wilds of Derbyshire. The specifics of how I achieved it, I cannot remember but I do think at this point Mr C joined the foray and gave me the much-needed support I required. Tonight, is the first occasion we have met up again after the jellyfish mission. We have been back in the UK for about a month and have returned to the apartment for a long weekend.

The sporting event on the TV has finished and it seemed that there was some unseen hand of fairness involved on these occasions because if France won the event, then England would win the next and so forth. It was gone 23.30 and looking directly at me Laurent asked, "Shall we have some muscles?"

Under normal circumstances my response would be either yes or no, depending upon my level of hunger at the time of questioning but you have to realise this is Laurent we are talking about and I am just a little bit wary of what I might be letting myself in for. I have watched with fascination the

107

locals wandering down to the beach at low tide with their buckets and scissors and marvelled at their knowledge and wisdom on knowing where to find these crustaceans and release them from their beds. Does he want us to meander down there at nearly midnight and give us a lesson in their collection? It is obvious that I am struggling with some inner conflict so he said, "From the restaurant we can have muscles and Mr C can have scallops."

Oh, yes, please.

So, off we trotted in a mini crocodile down the stairs out of the apartment block through the lawn area and into the side entrance of the restaurant garden, where Laurent uttered significantly, "Look out for holes and cats."

Strangely enough we have not been attacked by Ninja felines emerging stealthily from their subterranean hollows but have entered the garden unmolested. Situated at the bottom of said garden is a large shed that houses the restaurants seasonal workers in the summer.

"Look, I want to show you something!" Laurent exclaimed while opening the door to the shed. I have always wanted to see inside. I have always been a little curious to see how they lived in there but it is a bit disappointing to say the least not to see rows of bunk beds as the sleeping arrangements. *They must just bed down on the floor*, I thought, because I was being distracted by the lack of divans, I did not immediately see the object of our diversion. At the other side of the door were two large metal containers full of baby jellyfish.

Oh, no.

We have made all the expected oohs and ahhs. Well, I hope we have and I have to say we are more than a little relieved to see that there would be no more coercion of us to become surrogate parents. Thus, happy and content proceeded to the restaurant to cook our supper.

Thursday, 23 July

I have been invited out!

I was just sitting out on the balcony when Laurent called up on his way to the *Creperie* for the lunch time service to see if I would like to go with Sophie in the afternoon to the *Braderie*? Laurent was the purveyor of this request as he speaks excellent English and Sophie does not. Well, she does not speak any and why should she?

Sophie and I have had a couple of interactions over the last couple of summers. She is the seasonal chef at the *Creperie* and when the takeaway pizza place was situated under the apartment last summer, she was the main cook there. She is very bohemian and I think is quite active in the gay community. How I came to this conclusion? I do not know, but I think I am right. We have several different ways of communicating, for instance, whilst awaiting our pepperoni takeaway I noticed an ingredient, *cornichons*, for a different pizza listed on the menu and was confused as to what it was. I asked in my best French and pointed to it on the list just to make sure, whereupon she disappeared into the back returning triumphantly shaking a jar of gherkins in the air.

Earlier this summer she arrived for her three-hour lunchtime shift with her pet dog Tatin in tow. A great many people call their dogs this name, which seems a little strange to me as it is the name of a tart. I suppose it is the equivalent of Spud. Tatin is a griffin type dog, a large, black, lollopy, curly-haired specimen, which she was leaving in the back of her van while she performed her chef duties. I was obviously a little concerned about this proposed activity as the day was quite warm and the thought of him being confined in there for the duration was just not on and I clearly could not have this happen so I called down in my best French that I would look after him for her. She must have understood what I said, even though she was looking at me with an equal measure of amusement and annoyance and as she was bringing the excitable creature up the stairs to the apartment, Laurent appeared from out of his flat and said with some surprise, "What are you doing?"

Sophie, whilst looking askance at me and I must say a trifle dismissive replied, "She is looking after Tatin while I am at work."

Laurent raised his eyebrows slightly and Sophie responded to the look with "Yes, I don't know how they are going to get on because he doesn't speak English and she definitely doesn't speak French." Bit rude.

To which I said with a bit of aah, ah in my response, "No, but we both speak dog!"

She must think that my language skills have improved, the French, not the canine, because the other day when Mr C arrived with the kids for the weekend, his arrival coincided with hers. With a great flourish, which really impressed the kids, he told her who everyone was and how long they were here for. After a moment when she regarded Mr C with considerable distain and not a little irritation, she turned and looked directly at me, raised her shoulders and asked, "What did he say?"

So, we are off to a *braderie*, which is a grand yearly street market, mostly held in the summer months where local vendors put stalls up in the street outside their shops and sell their goods at a reduced price. As well as theses stands there are outside traders, food vendors, flea markets, art stalls and people dressed in traditional garments. The one in Morlaix was just the same, although I did not see anyone in traditional garb.

We wandered around, Sophie, myself and Jacque, the waiter, the latter, who wants a new pair of jeans which has found on an appropriate stall. What has followed is some sort of negotiation with Sophie siting on the vendor's chair, casually smoking whilst Jacque has scurried behind the stall to try on a pair of denims with a ridiculously narrow waist. He has decided he likes them and the previous arbitration between Sophie and the vendor has brought forth a glittery belt and a pink t-shirt included for the price of the jeans, which Jacque seems very pleased with.

I have followed them both around quite happily, although very quietly and a bit confused because of the language issue until my mood became more positive by someone in the crowd actually saying, *"Bonjour"* to me and not the others. It is the owner of a restaurant we frequent, but still, it is a person who actually recognises me. Whilst I am still feeling elated, we have met up with the summer chef who works with Sophie at the *Creperie*. She had her husband and numerous offspring following in her flamboyant and formidable wake. Each one of the joining ensemble have looked at me with curiosity and then have proceeded to completely ignore me. I have dutifully followed behind the considerably large group without having any clue as to what they are talking about. They are speaking incredibly fast and in some sort of local dialect. They have eventually stopped at a food vendor and proceeded to ask for various delicacies, which, of course, I have absolutely no idea of what they are, whereupon the summer chef turned around and shouted, "*Oi Anglais*," whilst shaking a *chicco* in the air at me. This is her way of asking if I want one. Very kind of her but just a tad embarrassing as this exchange has of course resulted in most of the food market spinning around to get a better vantage point to stare at me while I responded with a meek *'non merci'* whilst hoping the ground would open up and swallow me.

Xynthia

Monday, 25 January

I do not believe there are adequate words to describe leaving my adult children behind, even the expression adequate feels like a term that betrays the true depth of feeling in that moment. Some people will comment on the fact that they are 'adult', which should present the situation with a different perspective that they had their own lives, that they were not being abandoned. The truth is that at that point of departure, I feel that is what they felt and as a mother no matter how rational or level-headed I behaved, I felt it too. I will try to express how I felt but I honestly imagine whatever words I write to convey that sense of complete and utter loss will never truly reflect those feelings. I suppose you could compare it to grieving but no one had died to loss but what had been forfeited to defeat but what had been beaten?

The lead up to the point of departure had been a melting pot of opposing or complimentary emotions. It seems a cliché to describe it thus, but that is exactly how it felt. The excitement at a new adventure, the quest to understand all the bureaucracy attached to buying a house in France. The painstaking, boring, methodical sorting of all possessions into coherent, identifiable assets, rubbish and purely personal but essential effects. Constant communication, written and oral for all existing, planned and future services balanced against the ball-breaking (ironic) male chauvinistic attitude of French processes and procedures. The stress and worry of having to find nearly 25,000 euros extra in agency and notaire fees, after the expressed pride and smugness in ourselves at being savvy, knowing, seasoned buyers to the endless dump runs and charity donations that could have generated some supporting funds if we had planned things better.

All this noise amidst a non-acknowledgement of any personal or emotional effect, this process may be having internally on me or on any family member around. Until the inevitable explosion of pent-up anger, betrayal and incomprehension led to an all-out, no holds barred screaming, shouting, sobbing, expulsion of passion and emotion.

It is strange to reflect that although there were a multitude of words spoken, screamed or shouted and a host of conflicting and wide-ranging emotions expressed, not once did any of us say what was really at the bottom of it all. As a family our best form of defence is to attack, that is our modus operandi and to be fair I was always trying to display a positive façade. It was easy to do so when people were joining in the overall excitement and exclaiming such reinforcing sentiments such as "Oh, I wish we could do that", "I've always wanted to live abroad", "how lucky you are" and "how exciting". It was easy to go along with the supportive encouraging statements. It was not until a family member, not within the cauldron of passions, who professed 'not to be very good at this' said, "We will miss you." did the wall I had built and was hidden behind come tumbling down.

Wednesday, 24 February

How annoying is that?

It is my own fault. I just cannot help making assumptions and those hypotheses are grounded in my English experiences but get a grip, because you are not in the UK now, Mrs C, you are in France.

After my health scare and deciding to leave the apartment in Finistere to look to buy a permanent home in the beautiful Vendee, I did most of the research on the internet. I looked into areas, types of houses, access to airports and ferries etc. and so I think I must have known every house available.

A fantastic tool that I utilised during that time was Google Earth. I know some people felt like it invaded their privacy and that people could see them having a wee or something but I found it remarkable. It allowed me to look around the streets in the different areas without having to pay to visit those locations and so it gave me a good idea before we went to see any of the houses what facilities there were.

I am talking as if I was interested in hundreds of houses but from the beginning of the search, there was only one place for me, and luckily, Mr C felt the same way and that house was the *maison* we ended up buying, this one.

Now, as much as I love Google Earth, on this occasion it has let me down. I need to make it clear that it is not so much the fault of the application but on my own expectations based upon the assumptions I made using the tool.

I have just been up to the local shop. We have only got one, which is situated on the main street. Also, on the *Rue de Jaunay*, the main thoroughfare of Martinet are other notable points the Hairdressers (with room for a single client) the Mairee, the Iron Mongers, the Garage and most importantly, the bus shelter.

It was about the latter that I was visiting the shop. I had found out previously that this establishment was run by a French lady, Emmanuelle, and her partner, in the shop and in life, Mark, who is English.

I had been practising my best French as I had walked up the hill and as I entered, I saw who I presumed to be Emmanuelle (I was correct), standing behind the counter, and I said, "*Bonjour, je suis Mrs C, et nous achetons le maison de John et Maude* (Hello, I am Mrs C and we buy the house of John and Maude)."

"Oh, hello," she responded in English. "I thought you were French. There are not many English people who speak French as soon as they enter the shop."

I think she was being polite, seeing as how I can only converse in the present tense, no past or future and do not get me started on conditional and unconditional, imperfect and perfect, I do not even know what they are in English.

"Thank you, that's very kind. I thought I would come up and say hello," I expanded.

At that point a man entered the shop from out of the back of the units and the fridge freezer.

"This is Mark," explained Emmanuelle.

I smiled and performed the usual pleasantries. I explained who I was, about buying the house and a bit of general chit chat and then I expounded on why I had really ventured up the hill.

"I've come for a timetable."

"Timetable?" queried Mark considering Emmanuelle, both staring back at me with a blank look.

"For the bus," I offered for clarification.

"The bus?" they replied in the form of a question.

By this time another customer had entered the shop and Emmanuelle had retreated from our obviously confusing conversation and had gone to deal with her requirements.

"Yes, the bus," I repeated because me keep saying the same word over and over again was obviously going to aid the understanding on Mark's part.

"I don't know what you mean," came the response.

No kidding. I had had lots of situations in France where the French had real trouble understanding me but never with an English person, so I resorted to what I normally did in these situations and said very slowly and precisely, "The bus."

He looked at me as if I was mad, which, quite frankly by this time, I was starting to think so myself. "Yes, a timetable for the bus that stops at the bus shelter," I said in desperation.

"Oh." He smiled. At last, the penny had dropped, he laughed and he stated helpfully:

"Oh, yes, well, we've had a bus shelter for six years but we haven't got a bus."

Saturday, 28 February

Holy cow, I was not prepared for that.

I was aware of many things when we picked up sticks and moved here permanently, the most prominent of these considerations was that I would be one my own for long periods of time with Mr C remaining a majority of the time in the UK to work. There have been many practicalities that I was not ready or even knew about when we took up residence, like the electricity.

We were all exhausted when we arrived after two days travelling with all our worldly goods in tow. Phil, our good friend, had driven one van and Mr C the other. The house was absolutely freezing when we arrived and after making sure we had the sleeping arrangements sorted, we had a couple of glasses of wine and retired to bed exhausted. Phil even kept his woolly hat on all night. The problem when we awoke was how to heat the house when the electricity kept switching off. The damn thing would just not stay on and kept tripping out. In desperation I rang John, the vendor, and he suggested we spoke to Richard and gave me his telephone number. Richard very kindly came around to try and sort it out but apart from showing us where the fuse box was, so we could replace the fuses that kept blowing and ominously tell us the house has a mix of English and French wiring, so could not locate the problem. The issue was finally resolved when I noticed that the kettle with a French two pin plug had been put into a three-pin adapter back into a two-pin socket, sorted.

This did not really improve the heating situation as the stand-alone heaters we had brought with us only seemed to keep you warm if you stood in front of them while anything behind was frozen. Some relief was found when Richard demonstrated how to get a really good fire going in the log burner, although I was actually terrified we were going to burn the house down.

I just was not expecting it to be so cold and the first week I am alone I awoke to find a strange edifice in the garden. When looking out of the kitchen window I could not quite figure out what it was? I even rubbed my eyes convinced that they were playing some sort of trick on me but, no, it is still there and it looks uncannily like a six-foot ice sculpture is in the middle of the patio around the pool. Further investigation revealed that the pool shower has a burst pipe and as the water has hit the cold air, it has frozen immediately, the temperature outside is minus ten.

What to do? Turn the water off was my first reaction. How?

I have no idea where the stopcock is and I do not want to have no water whatsoever while I am on my own for a week but I really need to turn it off. An exhaustive search of all the appropriate and, to be honest, quite ridiculous places a stopcock could be produced nothing remotely useful in turning the water off. Unfortunately, I have rung the vendor John again. He is probably getting a bit fed up of me but I managed to determine from him it is in the secret garden under a huge flagstone and have gone to investigate with John's warning in my ear, "be careful, it is heavy and watch out for frogs."

Frogs?

It is ridiculously heavy and my first attempt has proved futile in moving the flagstone but needs must I have got to do it, so pulled with all my might on the orange rope attached to it and realised what John means by 'frogs' is actually rats.

After my herculean efforts to lift the stone boulder and a jumpy encounter with a French rodent – I hate rats. I was presented with a further hurdle. The stop cock is in a hole under the removed flagstone about four feet down. I am five feet. I somehow lowered myself down gingerly, lying flat on the cold, damp floor with my feet on the outside of the hole like some kind of human butterfly clip. I am literally balancing upside down with my head in a pit, trying desperately to turn the tap off whilst being uncomfortably aware that my face is next to the gap where the rat has just exited.

"The eastward-moving Atlantic storm dubbed 'Xynthia' left devastation in its wake as it passed through western Europe at the weekend, leaving dozens dead and half a million without electricity."

When the internet report says that it was western Europe that includes here. I am getting used somewhat to the cold. I was not really expecting it to be so chilly but it is what it is. This, however, is something else. It happened last night and I can honestly say that I have never heard noise like it, talk about scary, we are 25 minutes by car from the coast and we could clearly hear the sea roaring. It was impossible to sleep and I just lay there thinking, *well, this house has stood for 150 years, so hopefully it should be fine* and it is. Unfortunately, that was not the case for many others.

President Nicolas Sarkozy visited L'Aiguillon-sur-Mer on Monday, where he mourned 'a national catastrophe, a human drama with a dreadful toll' and said, "The urgent thing is to support the families who have people missing or dead. Sarkozy unveiled three million euros of emergency funds available for the victims and promised that electricity would be restored by Tuesday."

L'Aiguillon-sur-Mer is just down the coast from where we live and the poor inhabitants there bore the brunt of the storm.

The sea wall protecting the town was destroyed, so the water rose quickly as the people slept and they drowned in their sleep. Those poor people, there were over 50 souls who died. The majority of the houses in this region are single bungalows and many are fitted with electric shutters for extra security. Unfortunately, this quest for safety proved fatal. As the sea rose and swiftly entered the homes, those people who were not killed in their beds tried to escape but the electricity shorted the shutters and so could not be opened, so they frantically tried to reach the loft space in the roof but their efforts were hopeless and they drowned.

I did not sign up for this. I never in all the planning and preparation believed that after a month of living here, there would be a cyclone that triggered a mini tsunami.

We are so lucky; those poor people were not.

Sunday, 28 March

Six foot two and three quarters.

They were the first words Rich ever spoke to me as Jemima and I were waiting in the foreign currency queue at the post office. He had joined the line behind us un-noticed until Jemima turned around and saw him and animatedly introduced him to me as I looked up at him, I said, "Blimey, you're tall."

The rest is history as they say and Jemima and Rich have been together for some time now, setting up home in a nice little flat just before we moved to the Vendee. It seemed natural and right that they should be the first to visit us. It just felt imperative to me that they should probably because Jemima is my 'baby'.

We have been to pick them up at the airport, given them the tour of the house, put their cases into the studio, their sleeping accommodation and settled down for an evening meal, a couple of drinks and a catch up on all the family news and goings on. It has been a lovely evening and now it is time for bed but they seem a bit hesitant and instead of going out through the French doors in the lounge across the awning and into the studio, they seem instead intent on hovering around the closed curtains. It is not as you imagine that they are young and giddy and wanted to stay up drinking to all hours, quite the opposite really. Mr C and I are the rowdy pair. It is something to do with actually going into the studio, which became evident when Jemima turned to me and said, "Mum, will you just check our room please?"

"What for?"

"Well, I would just like you to look please," she replied a little sheepishly.

"What am I looking for?" I enquired, slightly amused.

"Bad men and badgers," she declared.

"Badgers!" I exclaimed, at which point Mr C joined the fray, laughing whilst enquiring incredulously. "Do you think you are going to find one sitting on the sofa doing a bit of knitting?"

At which point we all laughed but I have been in and searched the whole place for naughty Homo sapiens and errant nocturnal mammals, of which I have found neither.

This night-time search became the norm, including last night. Their final evening of their sojourn. I went and performed my quest, even looking under the bed, then kissed them both goodnight, re-entered the lounge through the double doors, locking them behind me, closing the curtains and settling down for a nightcap with Mr C. We were chatting away quite happily when there was a knock on the French doors. I looked a little puzzled and enquired of Mr C, "Why don't they just come in? They have got a key?"

"I don't know," he responded, "maybe they thought we were up to something."

I walked across the lounge floor smiling to myself. Yes, Jemima would be mortified if she had walked in on us and caught us 'al fragranti'. I opened the curtains and unlocked the door to find Jemima stood there dressed in her pyjamas awaiting me.

"What's the matter love?" I enquired.

"There's a snake," she replied.

"What?" I questioned.

"There's a snake," she repeated, "in our bedroom."

"Jemima, there is not a snake in your bedroom. It's March, they don't come out in March," I explained half-exasperated, half-amused.

"Well, this one has," she replied triumphantly.

"Oh, for goodness sake!" I exclaimed as I trailed behind her into the studio and asked, "Where?" as I followed the trajectory of her pointed finger.

"There," she announced with a clear 'I told you so' demeanour.

Halfway up on the wall above the bed was a five-inch worm.

Mr 'six-foot-two and three quarters' was laid in the bed, covers pulled up under his chin in an effort to repel any marauding earthworms, whilst also pointing an accusing finger at the unsuspecting giant serpent crawling up the wall.

I looked silently from one to the other, went outside to get a broom, returned, retrieved and re-patriated the wild troublemaker back into the garden and closed the studio door behind me.

Thursday, 24 June

We come a cob a coaling for bonfire night,
Your coal and your money we hope you enjoy,
Frol-a-dee, frol-a-daa, frol-a-diddle-I-doo-day,
Done in yon cellar, there's an old umbrella,
And done in yon corner, there's an old pepper pot,
Pepper pot, pepper pot, morning till night,
If you give us nowt,
We'll steal nowt and wish you goodnight.
If you haven't got a penny, an'apenny will do,
If you ain't got an 'apenny, then God bless you.

I have had this rhyme in my head for the past week.

We have been living in the Vendee now for five months and the only people we have really spoken to are our next-door neighbour Adele, Emmanuelle and Mark at the shop and Susan and Richard. Therefore, when the latter asked us whether we were going along to the *Feu de Martinet* or *Feu de la Saint Jean* to give it the official name, we jumped at the chance.

The feast of Saint John is traditionally held in most of the parishes of France, originally it focused on the youth of the villages and any newcomers, usually teenagers and from this group a King and Queen of Youth for the New Year was chosen. This festival, conventionally featured a lot of music and started in the morning with the Mass of Saint John, followed by an evening vigil with a large fire. The fire was built with logs that the young men and women had gone to beg the previous days in every house. It ended in a nocturnal ball.

I had no idea whether this would be the case in Martinet but either way the manner in which it was described reminded me clearly of growing up in the north and the activity of 'logging'. This was where you went around with your friends to your neighbours for any old furniture or anything they had that would burn ready for bonfire night. The night before the lighting of the fire, you would pay a return visit to the same neighbours and sing the rhyme, 'Cob a Coaling' in the hope that they would give you a few pennies so you could buy some fireworks. So, the description of the *Feu de Martinet* reminded me of that happy childhood memory, the only difference was this was not November but June.

We had arranged to meet Susan and Richard at 21.00 but decided to be brave and go along on our own before meeting up. It is only across the road at the *Ouches de Jaunay,* which I suppose is like an English park with a large lake in the middle, with a lovely walk around it and a vast area of grass. On this meadow is built the bonfire to be lit later, to the side of which is a stage with a variety of children performers in medieval costume and around the perimeter of the field are various stalls selling sausages, crepes and the like. To the side of these is a makeshift bar, so that is where we headed.

The drinks menu is on a piece of paper tacked to a pole that made up part of the bar structure, you could have beer or a glass of Rose or Red wine, that is the extent of the choice.

Mr C said in his best French, "A beer and a glass of red wine please."

The barman regarded him with clear hostility and shrugged.

Mr C repeated the request, "A beer and a glass of red wine please."

Mr 'I'm a tad stroppy' looked at him aggressively and said, "A beer and what?" Followed by the obligatory shrug, a little more pronounced this time.

"A red wine," responded Mr C, omitting the 'glass' and the 'please'.

Nothing. Just a glare. At this point I joined the fray.

"A beer and a glass of red wine, please," I trilled beaming widely.

He looked at me with an expression that clearly conveyed that my request had made everything clear, not.

"Wine?" he grunted.

"Yes, for me, a red wine," I replied with hope.

Nothing.

By this point the realisation was setting in that we might never get a drink tonight, at which point another barman appeared and asked what we wanted. We were a little dubious that the whole process would repeat itself but Mr C replied with a little a hope and not too obvious exasperation, "A beer and a glass of red wine, please."

To which the second barman immediately presented us with our drinks and a smile. He could obviously see that we were slightly bemused by this transaction, to which he stated again with a smile while cocking his head in the direction of Mr Stroppy, "He's vendeen."

Oh, well, that obviously makes it okay then.

I just hoped that when we wanted the next drink, Mr Vendee was on his break.

We wandered around trying to decipher what on earth was going on with the performers on the stage but it was hopeless. We have not got a clue, so we meandered through the throng of people have come upon Susan and Richard. They were speaking to an old lady and a young girl, the latter who I gleaned was the lady's granddaughter. She did not speak English but she spoke French very slowly and precisely, so that we could understand, totally the opposite to Mr Stroppy. After a little while of chatting, she invited me to her house next Thursday at 14.30. She would come and collect me. How nice. It was obvious she knew I was on my own in the week as there no invitation for Mr C to my knowledge. I had never seen her before in my life, village jungle drums again, I suppose.

It started to get dark at about 23.15 and the crowd began to stand around the fire, along with the *Pompiers*, there for Health and Safety issues, to await the ignition. Before this happened, a young girl entered the arena riding a white horse and some kind of play was performed before she dismounted her steed and was imprisoned in the fire. As we had no idea of what they had been saying, other that she was a virgin, we made up our own story, helped by the fact that we had had quite a few drinks. We have avoided Mr Stroppy and gone straight to Mr Smiley. That is not entirely true as every time we have approached the bar. Mr Stroppy has glared at us and made himself scarce.

At 23.45 they lit the enormous bonfire; the air temperature was 32 degrees Celsius.

Thursday, 1 July

Whoa!!! Married for the first time at 72! 72!

Oh, my God. Just how does that work?

You are a confirmed bachelor, lived all your life in a small village in the Vendee and you end up married for the first time to a 64-year-old widow with two adult daughters, grandchildren and an aged mother. I am sorry to keep repeating myself about the first-time marriage but the mind boggles. It is not as though I am going to glean any more information after my initial research with the 'jungle drums' as I think there may be a language issue involved with any further investigation with the participants themselves.

On the dot at 14.30 Sylvie, the lady from the fete (the blushing bride) appeared at the gate. We made our formal greetings and I followed her across the road and around the corner to her house. Well, it is her house now but it actually originally belonged to her husband Giles. As we entered through the front door we walked into a kind of short, narrow hall which opened up into the kitchen. It is a typical French *cuisine*, dominated by an enormous dining table with about eight mismatched wooden chairs placed around it. As we turned left through a doorway, we were met with another table, three chairs and the elusive Giles. I had not met him before as he was not very well on the night of the fete. He rose gingerly from one of the seats and we made our formal greetings. He seemed a very nice man but unlike Sylvie he spoke at breakneck speed. It is obvious that my inquisitive behaviour (nosey) is not going to elicit any further information about this curious romantic interlude. I am not going to get answers to such questions as: Where did you meet her? How did you woo her? What on earth attracted her to you?

Sylvie gestured to a chair on the other side of the table and asked me if I would like a cold drink. I was desperate for a cold drink, apart from the fact that it is boiling hot outside, somewhere in the high 30s. I am all flustered at being in an actual French couple's house trying to converse with them, accompanied by some slither of intelligence and dignity, plus we are sat in some sort of conservatory, full of windows. I have to say I am struggling to present a calm demeanour when I am sweating like a pig. Whilst Sylvie went to fetch the beverages, I smiled at Giles, who did not engage me in any further conversation, thank goodness, and looked around me. To the right are two doors, I presume to the sleeping accommodation and straight facing me is a dark, cool, shuttered lounge (oh, I wish I was in there) with access via a large archway and another enormous, ornate dining a table and further chairs. What is it with the French and tables and chairs? At that moment Sylvie returned with a shallow cardboard box housing a variety of small mixer size cans of fizzy pop and I gratefully selected a Coca-Cola.

Then it started. The interrogation.

For over an hour they took turns to ask me questions to which I have tried to answer as best as I can, which on most occasions is just complete rubbish but I have persevered and to be fair to them, especially Sylvie, so have they. How it happened? I have no idea, but somewhere in the copious number of questions about family, friends, work, Mr C, a very surreal idea has taken hold of Giles, whereupon he animatedly left the table with great speed, considering his earlier movement and disappeared into the darkened lounge. After a great deal of rustling and confusion on my part, he returned to the table carrying a large tome under his arm. Somewhere in the melee of the enquiries and my dismal responses, he has made a startling discovery and has ceremoniously handed me the book, written of course in French on Economics and Social Conscience, with the confidence that it would be a very good read and I would enjoy it.

Oh,

Sylvie was not oblivious to the look of horror on my face and decided that it was a good time to take me on a tour of the outside. Thank goodness, I mean, how on earth would I start to decipher that? I have only just got to grips with the rudiments of food and drink and some name places and that is speaking not reading.

As we entered the garden, the heat hit us. I had thought it was hot indoors but this was another level. The garden is huge and very well-ordered and seemed to be dedicated to growing fruit and vegetables which are all neatly labelled with little flags. This is obviously Giles' passion. Once the horticultural tour was over, we headed towards the house and at the side of the conservatory door is a large plant pot filled with snails. Sylvie explained that as Giles is gardening if he comes upon any of these shelled molluscs, he throws them in the pot for Sylvie. At the end of each day these gastropods are collected, boiled, stuffed with garlic and frozen ready for defrosting and consumption at a later date.

To the other side of the conservatory door is an external staircase leading to a second-floor door. As I followed Sylvie as we mounted this *escalier,* she complained about the children screaming and laughing in the swimming pool in next doors garden. Oh, how I wished I was with them. The door opened onto a large room filled with beds and strangely enormous pot plants. Sylvie explained that the former was for when her family came to stay and the latter did not need a lot of water, so were ideal to be kept up there. I was a little concerned about the lack of toilet facilities for the night-time needs of her relatives and why you would need or indeed want vegetation in an under used external bedroom but as with a lot of my internal questions concerning this visit, they were destined to remain unanswered.

I had been here two hours and it was beginning to take its toll both physically and mentally, so I said my profuse thanks for the invitation and made my farewells. Sylvie was mortified. I could not go yet. I had not had my promised cup of coffee. For God's sake.

Luckily, we retired to the kitchen which was thankfully marginally cooler and as Giles and I sat at the kitchen table, Sylvie busied herself with making the coffee. As expected, this beverage was not the instant variety which I utilised but the genuine percolated article. What I had not accounted for was the accompanying snack. Oh, no.

I do not want to sound ungrateful but firstly, I have a slight, I suppose, phobia about eating with people I do not know and secondly, unlike many women, I unusually do not like chocolate desserts. Placed in front of me was a lovely old-fashioned flower decorated plate with a tall thin glass filled with chocolate mousse with fresh raspberries on the side. Sylvie explained that the presented sweet was homemade by her own fair hands and the fruit was home grown and picked especially by Giles. No pressure then.

It was delicious.

As we are sitting at the table conversing, well, to be honest, by this time my utterings are monosyllabic interspersed with grunts. I have realised I have been in this house for three-and-a-half hours. They have let me leave this time, armed with the enormous academic hardback balanced on my hip.

My brain hurts.

Monday, 26 September

"Get your arses in this bloody house."

I am stood in the middle of *Rue de Jaunay,* screeching, sweating and pointing my right arm indignantly in the direction of our house and what do they do? They just calmly lolloped up the spare ground next to Christophe's house, ears flapping as they gambolled like little sheep coolly past me and through the garden gate.

It is a good job, it is lunchtime or else they would have been squished under a car.

It is my own fault, I know. I never imagined when I shut them in the kitchen as James and Steph arrived that they would be small enough to escape through the cat flap and that the gate would have been left wide open. It was sometime before I had realised they were missing but were they not bothered? Oh, no, they have had a wonderful time running full pelt around the village.

"Solitude is fine but you need someone to tell that solitude is fine." – *Honoré de Balzac*

That is the thing. I am not lonely but I am alone.

For the first six months of living here I did not feel that, or it is maybe that I just did not acknowledge it or want to admit that after only seeing Mr C once a week for a few days, I need 'someone' else.

The first realisation was when I was in the bath and the phone rang. It was Susan and I had to ring her back as I did not make it to the phone in time.

"Hi, did you ring me?" I enquired. Stupid, really, I always say that even when it is obvious they have done so because I have just rung them back after finding their number calling me.

"You are going to hate me," came the reply.

"Why?" I asked a little amused and a tad worried.

"Well," she began.

Susan is in an email group of expats here in the Vendee and one of them had put an enquiry message into the group about a kitten. Apparently, the lady in question had been out shopping with her husband when they spotted the tiny white feline on a roundabout next to the dual carriageway. They could not leave the poor little mite, which she thought was about five weeks old and had been obviously dumped there by some heartless individual. This was determined by the fact that there were no houses or farms around from where it could have wandered and so they managed to retrieve it. Unfortunately, they had a little dog that had taken an instant dislike to it, plus they were not permanent residents and did not want to go through the expense and 'faffing' around entailed in procuring a passport for it.

"Will you have it?" Susan concluded. "I can take you tomorrow to get it."

"Of course, no question. We will have it."

It did not enter my head what Mr C would think and when he made his routine night-time call, he was a little surprised and a bit apprehensive but to be honest, the decision was already made and so the first member of our extended family arrived. He has caused a few problems at first with being so tiny. He just looked like a tennis ball and he is profoundly deaf, many white cats are, that was probably why he was dumped. The issues arose from the fact that he developed a surprising knack of hiding in places that I did not even know were places like under the wardrobe and more disturbingly under the integrated dishwasher and around the back of the fitted kitchen units. It was no good shouting him either because he is as deaf as a post. It amazes me how he gets in there in the first place. The same conundrum as how the bat that lives under the awning can fly in, turn sideways and disappear into a gap in the stonework where the grouting has eroded, all in one fell swoop. We have called the cat Steve.

Steve settled in but that did not seem enough for me and once I had started getting pets, that was it. I wanted more. I have always loved animals from a small child. I even wanted to train as a vet at one point. Well, that and join a circus with a friend of my dad, who had a pony, seven dogs and a monkey. Consequently, I have always had pets from dogs, cats, mice, rabbits to terrapins and even a snake. I have to admit that was my brothers but I did used to 'borrow' it to chase the local children around the streets whilst the serpent was wrapped happily around my neck. I nearly inadvertently gained a further reptile as a pet earlier in this year.

I was weeding the flower bed under the roses as it was April. The idea of snakes hidden in the undergrowth never entered my head, of course the temperature here is different to the UK at that time of year but after the incident with the worm in the studio and my confident assertion that it was the wrong time of year for serpents, I just carried on regardless. I was in my own little world until as I lifted a clump of leaves. I accidently grasped the wriggling offender by mistake. What ensued I would imagine would have looked extremely hilarious from an interested onlooker's point of view.

I nearly jumped out of my shorts.

I threw the felonious interloper as far down the garden as I could, which proved to be not very far at all as I was doing that 'brrrrrrrrr' thing. Where I was trying to shake off every bit of the creature away from body parts that it had not even been near, whilst madly flaying my arms and legs around in what can only be described as frantic abandon, whilst simultaneously lifting my feet alternatively off the ground as far as my little legs would allow.

Snake bites are a bit of a problem here in France and they even have published information provided by Centre Antipoison, hôpital Salvator, 249 boulevard Sainte Marguerite, 13009 Marseille on the subject of Asp viper bites, (*Vipera aspis and Vipera aspis aspis*), the same advice applies to the Common adder, (*Vipera berus*). The one I picked up was a common adder. Unfortunately, at the time I did not know any of this and when recounting my story first to my neighbour, Adele, she just muttered, *"Viper"* in ominous tones whist constantly shaking her head. Whereas, when I recounted my exploits to Susan, she just told me matter of fact "Next time make note of the markings of the snake so that when we take you to the hospital, we can let them know which antidote they need to counteract the bite."

Blimey, it appears I was lucky.

So, snakes were definitely out. It appears that my time as a snake charmer had expired along with my youth. What I really wanted was a dog. Having a canine companion would make me leave the confines of the house. What I got was two.

For some reason I have always had a yearning for a West Highland White. I think it must have originated after seeing my old next-door neighbour actually dragging a reluctant fat rotund Westie up the main road for his daily walk. It was so comical and Jamie, the dog, was so sweet. So, I found an advert on *Leboncoin* for Westie pups not far away that would be ready for homing in a couple of weeks. So off we went and the rest as they say is history, Jack and Harry joined the family.

I feel I should have read the official West Highland White website before entering into this three-way partnership. "Westies should not be trusted off leash. They are likely to 'take off' oblivious to your frantic shouts."

No shit, Sherlock.

There Is a Hedgehog in the Pool

Tuesday, 24 May

I went to the market at Challans today. It has a market there every Tuesday morning, not to be confused with the fair that happens in July and August where the locals dress up in period costume from the 1910s and is known as *Autrefois Challans*, (Challans another time). I have never been to this fair as it is in the middle of the peak season and the town is absolutely heaving with people.

Challans, which is about a 30-minute drive away from Martinet, is the main economic centre of the Vendee and is the second largest town. It is known as the 'duck capital' and is associated with ducks in the same way the *Saint Gilles Croix de Vie* is linked to sardines.

I have been to the market before but today I am there with my sister and her husband. When we arrived and parked up, my brother-in-law went off to look around the garden centre and we have focused our attention on the market and the shops close by. We have arranged to meet up with him afterwards at the café on the corner of the market square.

The longer I have lived in France, the better my language skills have become. You might think that this is stating the obvious and that it would be an inevitable outcome but it is not always the case, take my sister for instance. I know they say that it is harder to learn a language in your 50s than when you are five, but my sister has been visiting this area for over 40 years and has owned a home for 20 years plus but she is hopeless. When she speaks to her French friends, she does not normally speak to the general populous, she utilises a not uncommon form of communication. She just says the English words slowly and loudly, in fact she shouts. I do not know whether her lack of acknowledgement of other French people is because of her appalling language skills or a generational reaction to 'foreigners'. I think it is probably a mixture of the two. Either way she fails to concede in any way that she is an alien in their country.

I am not a big shopper. I tend to know what I want, go and find it, buy it and then go and do something else. If I cannot find what I want, I do not go for hours going from shop to shop, I just give up. Oh, if only I could say the same for my sister! Even though we are in the second sunniest department of France with some fantastic beaches and other attractions, her idea of a perfect day is wandering around the shops and if there is a market, then she is in heaven. Unfortunately, because I cannot drive when she is in France, she spends six months here and six months in the UK she takes it into her head that I have to be 'taken out'. Unfortunately, this 'treat', however, always revolves around shopping. Well, actually she never usually physically buys anything. The trip takes the form of her taking the lead, venturing in and out of what appear to be random shops, stopping at various market stalls, explaining about this and that and then moving off with me trailing behind her saying things like "Oh, yes, very nice", "mm, they would be really useful" and statements of the same ilk.

And today is no different.

Halfway through this form of torture and part way up the main market street she espied something she wanted to look at. There was a young man stood behind a small table, not like other the normal market stalls, more a makeshift affair as though he is not normally there, not one of the regulars. On the counter are about 30 bottles of nail varnish in various colours.

"Oh, I've seen these before in England." Enthused Esther.

"*Bonjour,*" said the man hopefully.

"*Bonjour,*" I replied politely smiling. My sister on the other hand ignored this greeting, in fact she completely ignored the man. It was as if he had not spoken. She then said to me, "I don't think it is the same stuff."

"Oh, okay," I stated mechanically.

The salesman quite rightly determined from this exchange that we are English and changed his sales pitch accordingly and said in English, "Come closer, ladies, have a good look."

"*Non, merci* (No, thank you)," I replied moving away.

Esther remained where she was but again she completely ignored him and said to me again, "No, it's not the same."

At this point a young French lady approached the counter and the salesman in true retail fashion was not going to give up on a potential sale so started speaking and demonstrating his product on the French girl while beckoning Esther to watch the display. Again, as before she totally ignored him, turned around and walked away towards me and as she did, the salesman said under his breath, "*Bâtards anglaise ignorants.*" (Obvious what the translation is).

In a split second something happened to me. I do not know whether part of me agreed with him. My sister had been incredibly rude because she did not understand what was being said to her and thought if she did not look at him, he was not there. Or was it because I was indignant at what he has called us or whether he has assumed that I have not understand what he has said.

Whatever it was, it happened in a flash. I span around like wonder woman and literally shot over to where he was behind the counter, still conversing with the French girl, went as close as possible to him and whispered in his ear in my best French, "I understood everything you have just said." It was as if I had given him an electric shock, he could not apologise enough and just kept saying over and over again in French that he was sorry, while I marched purposely up the market towards my sister. When I reached her, I turned around and said in my best haughty English voice, "Yes."

What the hell does that mean? Of all the stupid things to have said, yes.

It seemed to do the trick though, the salesman was contrite and my sister looked at me as if I was a visitor from another planet and uttered in hushed tones, "I've never seen you behave like that before. You looked like you were going to hit him at one point."

I was definitely up for a fight. I think in hindsight it was because of my sister who is acting like the stereo typical English man/woman abroad.

We have not done any more shopping though, thank goodness.

Sunday, 17 July

When I lived full time in the UK, I worked with a man called Richard. It is funny when you are working, you get thrown together with colleagues with whom you have nothing in common with other than the shared environment and joint occupational subject. Well, Richard and I were two such people, never in a month of Sundays would you put him and me together as friends. He is very studious, serious and proudly academic to the point of quoting philosophers and trying to provoke intellectual debate and me, I am just not like that. In fact, people like that, get on my nerves a bit. It is like they are always trying to prove how clever they are or maybe I am just very insecure.

We used to go to lots of meetings where our joint attendance was mandatory. These gatherings were normally off site and sometimes quite some distance away and as I do not drive and Richard does, we would travel to these assemblies together. When I am nervous, I talk a lot and despite my own efforts, I always felt inferior to Richard, which made me babble on even more. I would engage in the inanest drivel and witter on about anything and everything that came into my empty stupid head, just trying to fill in the silences.

It must be at least two years since those embarrassing journeys, when out the blue I got a text message:

"Hi, hope you are well, thinking about buying in France. If you are around, how about a coffee or a cognac, Dickie?"

Who the hell is Dickie?

Mr C shed light on this puzzle, "It is Richard."

No!

You must be joking, never in my wildest dreams would I have called him Dickie. Mind you that is just like him, a Cognac!

Anyway, to cut a long story short, we started exchanging e-mails. It appears he had listened to some of my waffling on, which I think is quite an accomplishment on his part. I do recall that he had said on one occasion that he wished he could do what we were planning to do, go and live in France.

I remember replying quite astonished, "Why can't you? What's to stop you?"

Well, nothing, it appears because he has indeed bought a holiday home in France with the intention of testing the water as we did with the apartment to see whether he could settle out here for good. The house is in Brittany and as we just happened to be in the vicinity for my birthday reminisce and he had invited us to visit, we decided we would pop in, ex-pats and all that, to see how he was getting on.

It is another beautiful Breton July day, wet, cold and grey. We found the house quite easily, partly because we know the area a little and partly because of Richard's detailed directions, I would expect no less.

The house is positioned in a small hamlet of around eight houses, just off the main drag, nestled in a little dip. From the top road it looked in good condition. It appears to have a new slate roof and the design of the house is typically Breton, not unlike a house you would draw as a child, single storey, with the door in the middle and a window either side. As we pulled up onto the muddy drive, two things happened simultaneously. Richard appeared as proud as punch out onto the path and I realised that the cottage is not in as good a condition as I had first thought.

We live in a 150-year-old house, so we know the challenges of residing in a less than modernised abode but this is something else. As you entered the dilapidated front door, to the left is a small anti room which was dominated by an enormous, extremely dusty antique welsh dresser, the floor is covered in bits of stone, concrete, sand and what seemed to be mountains of dust. This 'theme' carried on through the rest of the house, such as it was. We moved from the anti-room into a large room, which I presumed is the lounge, dining room and kitchen and that is where that resemblance ceased. To support my assumption is a cooker, which is not connected to electricity or gas, a wooden table and four chairs and that is the minimal nod to living accommodation. The remainder of the room contains a jumble of what appeared to be random objects from lawn mowers to piles of bricks and everything but everything is filthy. I only knew that the table is wooden because I could see it's legs as the top of it is littered with plates, cups, bags, spanners, nails, jam jars containing anything from screws to plastic knives and forks and everything but everything is covered in a thick blanket of dust.

At this point, Jane, Richard's wife, descended the curved staircase in the corner of the room. She was not what I had expected. I had never met her before and to my knowledge Richard had never ever mentioned her to me, she seems very shy and reserved.

"Would you like to see the rest of the house?" Richard asked us.

"Yes, please," I replied politely. It was like some kind of horror movie you did not want to watch but you were fascinated all the same.

Richard then led us into a parallel room through a doorway. There is no door, into a concrete floored, breezeblock construction.

"Jane is very happy. We've not been able to have a shower for eight weeks but now we have this," Richard stated proudly.

Well, Jane is bloody bonkers.

There in one corner is a modern shower unit and in the opposite corner is a toilet and a bucket.

"Oh, and we have got a toilet but it's not plumbed in yet."

I did not have a response for that, nothing I could think of would be appropriate, so I just carried on with my, 'Oh, yes' and 'Nice' replies that I had been uttering since we arrived.

He then walked back through the lounge and conducted us up the stairs. At this point I was overcome and even my yeses and nice responses would just not come out, I was struck dumb, very unusual for me. The upper floor, if that is what you can call it, is under the eaves and runs the full length of the house, which it has to be said is not very long. On the floor in front of us filling the floor space are two tents, one with sleeping bags visible and the other one with clothes tumbling out onto the floor.

"That one is our bedroom and that one is our wardrobe." Richard pointed helpfully.

"Oh," I replied in a small voice as I turned to descend the stairs to be greeted by an owl winking at me from one of the many holes littered amongst the supporting gable end.

Once down the stairs Richard performed his host duties, Jane just sat and looked at us and he offered us a cup of tea. I was tempted to refuse but that would have been rude but I did draw the line when he asked if I wanted a piece of cake as he used a plastic knife, quite inefficiently to cut into four pieces, a small strawberry tart meant for one serving.

"Oh, no, thank you, Richard. I have just had a big breakfast," I replied rather sarcastically if I am honest.

I am not a big tea drinker, my beverage of choice being coffee or red wine and this cup was disgusting. The mug looked like it had never been washed, the white glaze inside being as brown as the true colour outside and it tasted of dust, no surprise there but I persevered as Richard held court. Jane has still not uttered a word but has just gazed in awe at Richard. I think there is something wrong with her.

He pompously told us how he spent the time of day with the local farmer, how all the neighbours thought his French is excellent. Of course, they would and how they always visited the nearer village rather than the larger town as it is more authentic. He is getting more pompous by the minute.

"We had a humbling experience the other day when we went on an outing to the village," stated Richard.

"Oh, yes," came my now automatic reply.

"Yes, when we came back, we realised how honest people are around here, as we had gone out without locking the door," he explained.

Well, that is it. It is as if the dam has broken and I cannot hold it back any longer and I have started to laugh loudly, uncontrollably and a little hysterically, I think.

"But, Richard, you've got no glass in any of your windows."

Wednesday, 22 June

For goodness' sake! I know that I am not very good at this 'countryside' thing and I appreciate that I do not know everything about every animal that inhabits it but I am damn sure that hedgehogs are nocturnal. I cannot recall seeing one in the day, early morning or early evening, yes, but not in broad daylight unless of course a poor individual has been squished in the middle of the road. So why has one apparently just jumped into the swimming pool at 10.30 in the morning? It was not there when I hung the washing out. I can only have been five minutes but on my return from the linen line behind the shed, here it is.

What to do?

The swimming pool has become the flipping bane of my life. When I tell people we have a swimming pool, trying desperately not to sound like I am showing off I might add, they exclaimed, "Oh, how lucky you are" or "how wonderful." Well, I am not and it is not! That may sound like I am really spoilt but the reality of owning a swimming pool is a far cry from the thought of it. It is bloody hard work.

I suppose my initiation into the aquatic world of the '*piscine*' was hindered slightly by a few issues. The whole cleaning and maintenance conundrum is down to me as I am the one who is here the majority of time, so I was given an extremely quick tutorial on running the damn thing by someone who clearly had never done so in his life. I think he used to pay someone to do it for him. Added to that I am in no way a strong swimmer and am forever frightened to death of falling in the flaming thing, not a good CV for a pool attendant. And that is before I have even opened it up.

The pool is protected in the winter by a blue cover, secured at various points around the periphery by long bungie type elastic fasteners. These have an impeccable knack of tripping you up whilst maintaining a vice like grip upon the large screws holding them in place. The cover is removed by being rolled up by a least two burly men as it weighs a ton and placed in a corner of the garden until the end of the summer, whereupon the reverse procedure is performed. The screws are then removed from the surrounding patio with varying rates of success as they either tend to get rusted in place after six months in situ or bounce out like a demented ping pong ball whilst depositing brown water all over your face. Leaving a very awkward unresponsive screw in the ground is a recipe for disaster because after an undetermined time, it will decide to jump halfway out on its own accord, therefore, being an accident waiting to happen for any unprotected foot wandering that way.

Underneath the blue cover is a white mechanical shutter. This is used to close the pool in the summer evenings to stop any wandering animals or drunken humans falling in. It is this cover I open up every morning to let the sun heat the water and of course let whoever is here swim. The pool does have a heater but my 'swimming pool' lesson did not include any detailed instructions on this facility and I have to admit that my operating it is very hit and miss. It is some time, however, before I can perform this daily function following the initial opening of the pool after the winter as I have to clean the pool first.

Oh my God! I was just not ready for this process. When it is opened up, you imagine lovely clear glistening water with blue tiled walls and softly rippling soothing tones. Wrong. It is a dark, dank, filthy expanse of water infested with leaves, dirt, seeds, branches and various dead animals. I had been told mysteriously in my scant tutorial to expect the odd dead mouse, which there always are, but not the disgusting amount of dead bloated football like toads hiding in the recesses of the murky depths – dog pooh bags come in very handy in disposing of such lovely findings.

The cleaning takes days of fishing all the debris out on a flat sieve-like bat attached to a very long pole. The deep end is six-foot-six, which I cannot confirm is true or false as I never swim down that end. Once this is completed, I get the robot out to clean the silt off the floors and sides. Now I have a bit of an issue with said robot because it just does its own thing and only cleans where it wants to. It is supposed to clean in a figure of eight, it does not. This completely frustrates me along with the fact that you are supposed to be able leave it to 'do its work' but that invariably means that when you return after a period of time, it has become very attracted to a corner of the pool and will not leave it no matter how hard you try to persuade it. This then means that I have to get the manual vacuum cleaner out. This consists of the same long pole removed and then attached to a brush type implement which is in turn connected to a very large snake like series of pieces of plastic piping, which you have to link together resembling a giant children's game. The ensuing five or ten minutes sees me running in and out of the pump room (a shed really) turning several levers off and on until the temperamental implement decides to suck rather than blow. This inevitably sees me chasing the vacuum cleaner, which through the force of sucking in air has careered down the length of the swimming pool because I am always in the wrong place when the damn things decide to work correctly. If I am lucky, I just manage to grab hold of it before the long pole falls horizontally into the water, so negating the need for me to jump in after it.

It is not finished here, oh, no.

To be perfectly honest I would have been better studying a degree in Pool Maintenance than Business Studies. There are mysterious mechanisms that come in to play at this point PH and chlorine levels no less. I think it is very important at this stage that I get the chemical levels in the water correct considering the 'stuff' I have fished out and no one is getting an ear infection or worse on my watch.

Some people may say at this juncture, just empty the water out and refill it. A sensible option you would think, however, there are some salient points here that need to be considered.

Firstly, the cost. The lady who had the pool put in was a single mum with an eleven-year-old son and she did not feel comfortable going on holiday to the 'costas' but wanted her son to have that kind of experience so bought the house and had what can only be described as an Olympic size swimming pool installed. It takes a lot of water to fill it. The Vendee is the closest place to the UK that has good weather from May to September and has 240 days of sunshine each year and because of its microclimate is comparable to the Mediterranean coast of France. Consequently, water prices here are astronomical and are at least four times the price as in the UK I would say.

Secondly, I do not want to create an international incident by draining the chlorine-soaked water and flooding poor Christophe's allotment for a second time.

God only knows why we bought a house with a swimming pool in the first place. Well, actually, I do know. It was for the kids, which is quite irrational as they only visit once a year, so what do we do with it for the rest of the time? I do myself go in it but only down the shallow end, obviously but Mr C never goes in. He has a quite unusual relationship with swimming pools, either plunging headlong into hotel pools in drunken bravado or sitting around them on holiday drinking beer. He has been known to comment interestingly about fellow holidaymakers but this activity came to an abrupt end never to return when he mistakenly questioned why someone would wear a fur lined swimsuit in a hot country. The poor woman was in fact suffering from an unnatural, frenzied and untamed profusion of pubic hair.

One Sunday I broached the subject of Mr Cs apparent fear of the water. He said that he was not afraid just a little embarrassed as he was not a good swimmer. Neither am I.

I persuaded Mr C that he should at least try a bit of swimming and so it was decided that we would lock the gates so that any unannounced visitors could not inadvertently wander in and I would get in the pool with him for moral support in the shallow end, of course. As Mr C has never frequented swimming baths in his life and on hot days sunbathes in shorts and T-shirts so he does not have the relevant bathing attire, so he decided to enter the pool naked, which took some time due to the 'freshness' of the water. I was very encouraging I felt and suggested to him "Why don't you try and swim a breadth?" To which he obliged me and set off breast stroking across. When he reached the opposite side of the pool, something extraordinary happened. He went into a super doper forward roll, not unlike a professional swimmer with the obvious intention to proceed underwater in the opposite direction.

Well, the little bugger, I thought indignantly, he is a trained swimmer. He has been hiding this from me the whole time. It was at this point that I realised that he was not actually swimming back towards me but flapping wildly about under the water. I immediately went to him and pulled him upwards while saying with some exasperation "Stand up, you fool." He was after all only in three foot of water. He came upright spluttering and coughing and explained to me that he had not been performing a perfect body roll but had made a grab for the edge of the pool, missed it and was in fact drowning. It was a full 15 minutes before I could get out of the pool because I was laughing so hard and could not get the picture of his naked bottom and other bits and pieces bobbling about upside down.

What to do with the poor hedgehog?

I felt I had to move quickly, so I got the long pole with the bat like implement on the end and managed to scoop it out. It was still breathing. At this point I must admit I did flounder a little. I did not want to give it mouth to mouth resuscitation and although it was laid on its back and therefore presenting a smooth underbelly bereft of spikes, I did not want to massage it as I knew they are full of fleas. Besides which I did not know how to perform CPR on a hedgehog, so I resorted to blowing very hard in the direction of its mouth. Needless to say, my attempts at lifesaving were unsuccessful. I then had the matter of what to do with the poor creature, I hopefully texted family members in the UK for a solution and their replies I have to say were less than helpful.

So, I decided to bury it in the garden and I have to admit to shedding a tear in the process.

Tuesday, 4 August

I love living here and today was a reminder of why. Apart from the weather and the lifestyle, there are other things that makes residing here wonderful. For a long, long, time I have loved watching people, their behaviour, their mannerisms, their lives such as what I can see, maybe I am just a very nosey person. I love nothing better than sitting in a café, sipping a drink, watching the world go by. I fit in very well around here, the French are some of the most inquisitive people I have ever known. I do not think I am as bad as them though. I would never invade anyone's personal space and stare directly in their face, voicelessly enquiring what the hell they are doing but I do love to regard.

In the village there is a population of about 700 people between 10 and 20 of those are British. This number changes, dependent upon the time of year and season and whether the two that live facing the church are off doing their missionary stuff. The remainder are French, we have six houses near us, which I would regard as close neighbours and all of these occupants are of the latter nationality.

At the back of the secret garden, facing our house is the gable end of a bungalow. This is the holiday home of a family from Paris. Last summer when we were here, the grown-up son, daughter and grandson appeared at our gate, greetings were performed and then they just sort of stood there staring at us. I knew, from who knows where, that the grandson had previously frequented our pool with the consent of the previous owners and I also knew he was not accompanied by an adult. Having a swimming pool is such a big responsibility and as I am not a good swimmer by any stretch of the imagination, anyone going in it must either be a grown up themselves or have one with them and that person is not me. I do not want any drowning on my watch. As it was obvious that they did not speak English and our French did not cover poolside behaviour, we all knew the request was there but was left unsaid and dangling in the air and they left. Consequently, every time the grandson rides by on his bicycle when I am weeding the drive, he looks at me askance and I feel guilty and sad, all at the same time that he cannot come in and play. The bungalow owner's wife, the grandmother, is very pleasant. I have no idea what their names are and she says *Bonjour* when she sees me. The owner on the other hand pays me no attention whatsoever. There was one occasion when he has come into contact with me when he could not avoid it and he just grunted something at me. The only time I have been anywhere near their home was when I was chased up there by Adele's malevolent cockerel.

To the right of the secret garden is where Adele lives. I would describe her as a typical old country lady. She is 84, has a moustache and beard, her boobs are somewhere south of where her waist should be and she speaks patois. She has, however, a smile that would light up the whole house, never mind the room. We have a funny relationship. We always say hello if we see each other in the street, which is very rare, but for anything past that single word we adopt a filtration system through her grandson, Stephane. He has really good English, however, he refuses to speak it to me unless we are both at a standstill. He says that I can speak French and so I should, fair point. We obviously only use Stephane when he is around and available, otherwise if he is not, I have not got a clue what she is saying to me. On one such occasion after a long, detailed conversation with her, Mr C enquired, "What did Adele have to say?"

To which I responded, "Something about a black cat."

So, if I need to ask her something or I am invited around, I use Stephane as an interpreter. I speak my best French, whereupon he tells his Mamie in patois, where she replies in kind and then he tells me what she said in French. This seems to work well, except on one occasion when I was asked in for a coffee. I try not to get invited in, to be honest, I know that sounds awful but her house is absolutely jumping. Add to that, that bloody cockerel and I give it a wide berth.

Her house is all on one level and consists of three rooms, a lounge/dining/kitchen, a bedroom and a bathroom, at the entrance is a couple of steps up and a lean too affair which is full of pot plants and bowls of cat food. She was the farmer's wife until he died and is a true county woman. She has loads of cats which are half-wild and which she controls by, shall we say, old-fashioned methods, no inoculations, spaying or vets' visits, so they are absolutely covered in fleas and so is all her furniture.

I try and sit on one of the many mismatched dining chairs if possible, when I go around as these are wooden and a little bit more flea immune than the sofas. I find it really difficult to find subjects to discuss. We have absolutely nothing in common, from heritage to dialect, to beliefs, add to that the language issues and any conversation does not exactly flow. On the occasion in question, I had exhausted everything I could think of, even though Stephane bless him had risen to the occasion and brought up the subject of the donkeys. I love donkeys and we have a donkey sanctuary in the next village. We had discussed where they were, what they are called in French, how to get to them, what you could do when you got there etc.

So as the silence seemed to deafen us, I thought to myself, *animals seem to be a safe subject.* I thought, *Oh, I will tell them what I found in the pool, the hedgehog.*

To this day I do not know why I decided to discuss this event. To be very honest I did not even get onto any detail because we could not seem to get through the interpretive filter system what kind of animal I was talking about until Stephane in exasperation and slightly incredulously gave in and said in perfect English, "You have a pig in your swimming pool?"

Adele does not walk anywhere in the village. She has a little car that she uses for her excursions. These trips are largely dedicated to a run up the main high street to the shop for her daily baguette. She drives Emmanuelle mad; the shop is open in the morning from 7.30 till 12.30 but Adelle will invariably turn up for her bread at 12.30 and always but always parks her car across the entrance to the zebra crossing whilst knocking down the stand-up shop sign in the process. Unfortunately, for Emmanuelle, this behaviour is not just limited to Adele, no, Madame Bertrand, Adele's big pal, adopts this shopping approach also.

Madame Bertrand lives on the other side of our garden, with her house facing directly onto the main road. There are always one or two families in French villages that are the 'bigwigs', usually they have been successful in business and therefore are viewed as wealthy by their neighbours, Madame

Bertrand is one of these people. I have no idea what her first name is but I get the impression that it would be very 'informal' of me if I did know it to use it. In their heyday, they ran the garage in the village, owned several houses and an apartment in *Sables d'Olonne* and were part of the 'jet set'. Those days have long gone along with the running of the garage, the houses and the flat with the death of Monsieur Bertrand. The only time I see Madame is when she is going up to the shop or driving the hundred yards around the corner to visit her friend Adele, whereupon she parks her car on our drive.

The other three neighbours I see infrequently in the summer. I see Monsieur Albert more than any other time with his frequent visits to the bins but the other two I see rarely, although I feel their presence in two very diverse ways. Paul, who lives across the road from the bottle bank seldom makes a personal appearance to me but always appears when Steph visits, which secretly annoys her but I take the view that he is watching out for me, which is nice.

The last of the close neighbours makes me smile.

I do not know his name. I know he has a wife but I have never seen her and have very rarely seen him but I always hear him. He is a retired policeman, another fact gleaned via the village gossip facility and it appears that he has decided to learn to play the trumpet in his now leisure time. As the weather here in the summer is usually very hot he plays after lunch with the windows wide open and as is my want that is the time I am usually laid on the sunbed at the side of the swimming pool. He was really bad at first, the noise was excruciating but he is getting better to such an extent that now on some days I can even decipher the tune he is murdering.

It has become apparent to me over the past few weeks that there is some sort of concert or recital in the offing, which involves some other instrument playing individuals and that the practice session for this event is on a Tuesday afternoon. To be honest they do not sound that good really but I have to admit that the number of times I lift my shoulders up, drop my chin onto my chest and try to cover my ears as they run through the programme has decreased. The problem is they do always seem to get stuck in the same place in the same song and I find myself waiting with bated breath when they get to the pesky notes whilst silently willing them to get through it, which they never do.

Today is Tuesday and Jessie and Zach are here for their annual holiday. Whilst relaxing around the pool, the weekly rehearsal began. Oh, I wish I had my camera with me to record the expressions on the faces of Jessie and Zach because of the extremely sultry weather, the ensemble had decided to practice in the layby at the side of our garden.

Thursday, 8 September

Sometimes, just sometimes this place drives me mad!

I got up this morning and was following my normal routine when I heard voices outside the gate. We have an enormous metal double door gate, which to be honest has seen better days at the side of our house, which opens out onto the front onto what I call 'our drive'. As it happens, it is not ours and it is not a drive. It is a piece of land in front of our house which belongs to the mayor, however, he has never done anything with it and the previous owners of the house have reclaimed it bit by bit by putting gravel down and planting several trees, including a beautiful eucalyptus specimen.

To the left-hand side as you look out of the gate is a tumble-down building belonging to our neighbour Adele to call it an 'eyesore' would be a misrepresentation, a little too grand a description for what is actually there. It is a large lean to, with two low walls either side of a large gap which acts as a doorway, covered by which was once a tiled roof. This feature has long since disintegrated and is in fact a mixture of old broken tiles and rusty corrugated iron. It does have a guttering system of a kind, which is held on in several places by bricks and chunks of wood attached by dangling rope. I think she used to keep her wood in it but that function has long since ceased and it is now just an earth floored dumping ground for broken chairs.

To the right-hand side, our fence weaves along the side of the road towards the junction with the main village thoroughfare and straight facing the gate across the drive and the little road is the bottle bank and what used to be the public '*poubelles*'. These bins were there mainly for the visiting holiday makers in the campsite and gites around the village but have long since been removed when the council introduced a new refuse collection process. Unfortunately, that does not stop people dumping rubbish there still, much to the annoyance of my neighbours. The bottle bank remains and many a day when I am sat weeding 'the drive' (I cannot bend over as it hurts my back) people recycling their glass regard me with either derision or amusement, dependent upon their personalities. Monsieur Albert, who seems to dispose of bottles every day, will stop and have a chat with me on his way back home. As this usually consists of gardening tips, it is always a very one-sided affair.

I decided to investigate what was happening. As I opened and walked through the gate, I was met by a chattering crowd, which appeared to me to be a weirdly diverse group. The gathering consisted of my neighbour Adele, Brigitte and her husband from up the road, Christophe from off the main road with his grandchild sat in a pushchair, a random man in overalls I had never seen before pushing a wheelbarrow, another man in overalls with two children about 9 and 11, a man with a long metal pole and a smartly dressed man. Not a soul acknowledged my presence.

After a while as they continued animatedly jibber jabbering and completely ignoring me, I began to get a tad annoyed. They were after all stood on my drive. I decided to approach Adele to ask her what was happening, not the best idea I have ever had considering her penchant for speaking patois but needs must. I greeted her and enquired in my best French what was happening and from her response I could only make out one thing 'grey water'. Oh. Once she had imparted this information to me, she turned her gaze back onto the crowd and resolutely ignored me again.

It did actually make sense. When we bought the house, there was some concern about 'grey water', the water that drained off the land into the municipal drains. One summer when John and Maude, the previous owners, had been resident, they awoke to find the swimming pool a lovely dark pea green colour and no amount of cleaning could rectify the matter, so they decided they would have to drain it. They did not tell anyone in the village they were going to do this and consequently the old drains could not cope with the volume of water and sent a chlorine flavoured river tumbling down the high street. Many residents thought the village was going to be flooded and poor Christrophe found that his allotment bore the brunt of the deluge and that his poor fruit, vegetables and soil were completely ruined.

During the melee of raised voices, I gathered someone had gone to fetch the mayor. Oh, good, every village in France has one. I had never met this gentleman but knew a couple of random facts about him. Again I do not know from where, that he was not well liked, his wife was Scottish and his day job was as a teacher.

When he arrived, he said hello to everyone else but me and started to talk to several people in turn but completely ignored me like they all did. I was by now thoroughly annoyed. They were all on my drive, talking about my drains and not including me in any way, shape or form. I decided to take matters into my own hands and indignantly went over to talk to the mayor myself.

"This is my house, can you tell me what is happening, please?" I asked in my best French authority.

Now he could have spoken to me in English I know, but of course he did not and explained I think that the man with the pole was trying to find my manholes, so I responded a little smugly that they were in my garden. At this point on hearing my words, I must be getting better at the language lark, the whole ensemble minus Adele, Brigitte and her husband wandered past me into our garden, including the man with the wheelbarrow, how rude. What happened next was a bit of a blur, all the men started wandering around, picking up plant pots and generally discussing the drain situation with the exclusion of me whilst the two children ran around screaming and making a nuisance of themselves. Eventually, I explained to them in my limited French where the main holes were and how the water drained out of the garden, whilst the nice man with the wheelbarrow kindly replaced my plant pots and the other man in overalls removed the annoying children from out of the garden.

The situation was resolved when the mayor said he would write to someone, I have no idea who, to ask about drains and whether we needed another manhole in the corner near the garden wall. Or that is what I convinced myself he said to which I asked, as the Patron, which I was clearly not regarded as, not being a man, whether he would then let me know the outcome.

Whereupon he looked at me, shrugged and replied, "Might do."

Just What Are the Rules for Boules?

Wednesday, 20 June

"Don't judge a book by its cover."

Oh, how true this seems today.

For some time now, I have seen an individual around the village whom I presumed was a post person. Why did I believe this? It was because said person drives around on a yellow scooter, these vehicles being the transport mode for postal delivery employees. It was natural for me to assume that this was the case in this instance. I could not think what else it could be and apart from thinking that they must be very forgetful or new because they seemed to be traversing the same 'walk' or 'route' over and over again on the same day, ignored them from then on. A few days later I did think that perhaps this individual was a Pizza Delivery operative as there now seemed to be a large yellow box perched on the back of the vehicle. It was only on entering the shop some weeks later that I put two and two together and realised that the personality seated on a garden chair in the corner next to the magazines is the new lady in the village and the self-same busy potential postal or pizza delivery worker.

Sabine lived in Paris with her partner, Gabrielle, and it is Gabrielle who has bought a holiday home in the village; however, this damsel has not arrived at the purchased abode yet as she has work commitments until her regular two weeks' holiday in August but Sabine has been in Martinet a month now and planned to stay a further two. I do not like to generalise about people or pigeonhole them but if I had not known Sabine is a woman, I would have generally assumed that she is a man by her appearance. She has a large chunky frame, skinhead haircut and a love of male clothing which she buys predominantly from British shops. One of her overriding passions in fact is for anything English from clothes to music, to dogs, she owns an English Bull Terrier named Doris Day because she presumed by the name that all dog owners in England would possess this breed.

Some of this information was gleaned at that first meeting, Sabine's love of English does not extend to the language and she only speaks French, although I suspect she knows more then she lets on. So, it was speaking with her and gaining interpretation from Emmanuelle that this knowledge was had. I had also heard something about her through the village 'jungle drums'. I know on this occasion Emmanuelle had provided me with a lot of data, including that Sabine would arrive at the shop at 7.30 every morning and leave at around 11.00, which was fine at first but I think Emmanuelle was getting a bit fed up of the situation as the weeks go on. This is not helped by the numerous occasions when Sabine is heard to complain that it would be a much better ambience in the shop if a coffee machine was installed. I learnt that day that another one of Sabine's loves is Heinz Baked Beans.

I charged Mr C with the task of procuring a four pack of these delicacies while he was in the UK working and at the weekend he returned home with the goodies. That Monday morning, I went up the road armed with the tins and presented them to Sabine along with an Adele and Barbra Streisand CD. She was very pleased.

The following week I got an invitation from Emmanuelle to go to her house for a meal that Sabine is going to cook for us as a thank you for making her feel welcome, John and Sylvia have also been asked to attend as they had made friends with her too. I was a little confused as to why we were going to Emmanuelle and Mark's house but a night out in the week when I was on my own is definitely very welcome. Sabine cooked us a tradition Senegal Tagine. Sabine was brought up by her grandmother in Senegal. It was nice and very sweet. I do not think I would ever order it in a restaurant but it is very kind of Sabine to make it for us and we had a lovely evening, eating and singing. I did ask Emmanuelle directly about why we were there and not at Sabine and Gabrielle's and she said rather mysteriously that it was because they did not have six of everything matching at their house, which is very odd because the majority of French really could not care less about those things.

I found out the real reason a couple of days later. After her stint at the shop, Sabine had taken to calling at my house for a beer on her way home for her lunch. How she recognised that I was the kind of person that would offer her an alcoholic beverage at that time of day I do not know or she just may have assumed that I would because that is it what the French do, which was a compliment in one way. My morning activity normally consists of me arising around 8.30 and taking the dogs for a walk before it gets too hot, then returning home for my first cup of coffee. It would then entail some sort of decorating, garden maintenance or pool cleaning to be done before 11.00 because after that time the temperature is just too high for me to contemplate any manual activity until after 18.00 which never actually happens because to be honest by that time, I am usually having an aperitif. So, as it is my custom, I was just considering that I should eat something for breakfast when Sabine would arrive. As I have at this point an empty stomach, I can manage to get away with drinking water in my own home but it is a different matter when I am invited to Sabine's. She wanted me to come and see her home, so off we went.

Their house is only just around the corner, I knew, again I do not know how that it had been owned by the brother of Giles, who a confirmed bachelor in his 70s had died 30 years before and the house had never been lived in since. It is a traditional vendee structure which is directly onto the road, all on one level with a large gate connected to the end of the building, which is in turn attached to a double height old stone garage. The garden ranges to the side and the back of the house, now I say garden, it is more like a jungle. Apparently Sabine does not do gardening, that is Gabrielle's job and seeing as how she has not arrived yet, there is 30 years of growth to contend with. Sabine is very insistent that I examine this oasis in great detail, which is a little challenging to say the least considering I am dressed in shorts, t-shirt and a pair of flip flops. After wandering along the secret passage of fig trees and traversing the multitude of brambles and clumps of vegetation, whilst trying to avoid a broken ankle in the many potholes generated by Doris Day's penchant for digging for toads I was relieved and thankful for the offer of a cold beer, breakfast or no breakfast.

When I entered the building itself I could understand why Emmanuelle had been insistent that we ate at her house. The house consists of three rooms, where each chamber can only be entered into by going through the previous one. My immediate reaction when entering the first one is that it is a lounge, as it houses a sofa, a dining table with benches, an enormous fireplace and a table containing an extraordinary amount of computer equipment and the biggest TV I have ever seen. Further investigation revealed that there is a double bed in the corner and Santa is still climbing the internal chimney taking his sack of presents with him in the middle of June. Through a door to the right is the next room, which is a kitchen, I know it has that function as there is a cooker and a sink in there but that is the only indication to its purpose as the only other thing is an old wooden dresser which seemed to abound with blue paper packages. They looked as though the wrapping is nurse's scrubs.

Weird.

I have no idea to this day what they are. The final room is the bathroom. I did not even enter; it is enough for me to know that Doris Day sleeps in the shower. All the floors are plain concrete and what windows there are have the original net curtains belonging to Giles' brother, I do not know if they have ever been washed but I suspect not as surely they would have disintegrated if they had. I think the best way to describe it is rustic.

A few days after my introduction to Sabine's abode, she appeared in the garden. This fact was heralded by the amount of barking that was going on. Jack just did not get on with her, she tried so hard to win him over but to no avail. He loves Doris Day though. Today she was dog less and seemed in a bit of a flap. Sabine makes no concessions for my nationality or the fact that my French is very limited, she speaks at normal speed, very fast and takes no prisoners with her language. She just speaks to me as if I understand every word she is saying.

I could determine several things, she is upset. Well, upset is not the word. She is scared of something but what it was I do not know, she just keeps repeating the word *Frelon* over and over again. Oh, the irony. Also, that Emmanuelle had something to do with what was going on and so did I. Oh. Eventually, I understood that she is scared of this *Frelon* thing, she had told Emmanuelle and she had told her to come and see me as I was scared of nothing and I would sort it out.

Oh, thanks.

So off we went. On the way there I discovered this *Frelon* thing had appeared at 4.00 in the morning from since which time Sabine had not been able to sleep. As soon as I entered, she had me search everywhere, including behind the wardrobe, in the bed, under the bed, under the pillows and any other place she felt this thing may have retreated to, no *Frelon* was found. At this point she decided to show me some files on one of the many computers she had and I ascertained, how, I have no idea that she would copy me these files on to a memory stick as they would help me learn more French. While I was looking at them, she brought me a large tumbler containing about a centimetre of orangey liquid and handed it to me saying, "Do you like *troussepinette*?"

Taking the glass from her whether I liked it or not, because to not drink it was not an option. I said that I did not know what it was. It tasted very nice and very strong. Thank goodness there was only a small measure as I realised it was some kind of liqueur. I continued to try and understand what the files were that were miraculously going to engender my fluency in the French language when she returned with my glass again. I had not even realised she had taken it. This time it is full to the top.

"I can't drink that," I screeched. My God! I had not eaten a thing all day.

"Why not?" She shrugged. "You are on holiday, aren't you?"

Well, technically, I am not, but I do not have the capability in language or clearness of thought to explain the nuances of my stay in Martinet, so I replied, "Er, well, yes."

"And you haven't got anything to, do have you?" she enquired.

Well, not anymore, I thought but responded with, "Well, er, no."

"And you can have a sleep after, can't you?"

I did not try to explain that I am not French and I do not have a nap every day after my lunch but just gave in to the inevitable and said, "Yes."

Whereupon she looked at me with that 'well, what are you talking about?' look, shrugged again and continued to drink her beer.

Thursday, 19 July

I think that it is the best line I have ever heard since I have lived here in France.

This morning Sabine came to the house to see me. She normally arrives around 11.30, has a couple of beers and then goes before 12.30. The French are nothing if not creatures of habit. As usual I have not even had breakfast yet and she is ready for lunch.

We go through the usual, often performed, rigmarole whenever she arrives in the garden. Jack just does not like her. Harry on the other hand can take her or leave her but Jack, well, he is another story. This ritual always takes the same form. She bends down low with her hand held out, saying pleadingly with her deep baritone voice, "Jack, *c'est moi, c'est moi.*"

He knows it is her and that is the problem.

While she is pleading, he is running around just out of reach, barking and screeching like a wild thing with me chasing him, ending in the inevitable unsuccessful capture of a lively Westie and so, I resort to the usual ploy and squirt him with water from a washing up bottle. Eventually a wary truce is achieved with Sabine sitting sipping her beer, occasionally putting her hand down to entice Jack, while Jack, he is having none of it, grumbles softly and slowly under his breath.

"Are you going on the *rando* tonight?" she enquired when calm is achieved, well, sort of.

The '*rando*' is a walk which is organised in the summer by the campsite at *Les Ouches de Jauney,* whereupon hungry walkers set off on an 8 or 12-kilometre jaunt, dependent upon their hiking expertise with stops along the way to eat.

"No," I replied warily because I know bossy boots will have something to say about it.

"Why not?" she demanded and I mean demands, she can be quite scary sometimes.

"Emmanuelle has long legs, I am little," I replied in my best French. Well, you have to use the words you know and frankly, I just do not know how to say – Emmanuelle did ask me and I was going to go with her but Emmanuelle has really long legs and walks very fast, so fast that I can hardly breathe and I cannot keep up with her.

Uncannily she seems to understand what I said and she stated matter of fact, "You will come with me."

Now you have to understand, there is no debate. It is a statement, although said in the way of a question that brooks no argument.

That is it then we are to meet at the campsite at 18.30.

This causes me a bit of a fashion conundrum. The weather forecast says that at 18.30 it will be 26 centigrade (I have moved to the continental temperature measurement, like a duck to water), so a bit warm. We are going for the 12-kilometre walk, again no argument and flip flops and shorts are not really hiking attire, and that is the problem really. I am just not 'made' to go waltzing around the countryside in walking boots and cagoule. After great consideration, I plumped for t-shirt, jeans and flat winter boots, my feet are boiling.

I arrive at the campsite to find that there are six of us going to walk the *Rando*, phew, the emphasis will not be purely on me to speak French all the time. There are other people to take up the reins with Sabine. The others are my neighbours, Bill and Becky, John and Sylvia and Doris Day, Sabine's dog.

Doris Day is quite a big dog and very much like her owner, some people are scared of her. This is not helped by the fact she does not listen to a word Sabine says, strange seeing as Sabine is training to be a dog whisperer and Doris Day is often off her lead being disobedient. At this point she is on her lead, good.

So, we set off on the *Rando*, in straggles, with what seems to be half the village and more besides, while consulting our provided map for route clues. At the beginning of the walk this was quite unnecessary as there are so many of us going in the same direction. We just followed the people in front.

As soon as we left the village Doris Day, was let off her lead.

What ensued became a pattern for the first part of the walk until the first feeding point about four kilometres away. Sabine partnered up with John, both walked slower than the rest of the group and John spoke fluent French, so they were natural partners and at this early point relinquished all control over Doris Day, leaving her to roam leash less. I walked with the other three, sometimes we walked in twos but mainly the four of us continued together, but what was consistent for this part of the walk was the effort made by Bill, Becky and myself on keeping Doris Day under control.

The French have a very different way of treating 'pets', cats are in the majority regarded as 'outside' pets along with a great many dogs, which tend to live in kennels, tethered to a long rope or allowed to roam unchecked. The majority of French dog owners are either very strict and shout and beat their pets or laissez faire and let them run around regardless of the dangers or the annoyance to other people.

The arrangement that followed then was pretty constant and consisted of Bill, Becky or myself capturing Doris Day and putting her back on the lead, usually with me walking the dog, followed a couple of minutes later with Sabine catching us up and releasing Doris Day from her confines. This charade was repeated regularly until the first feeding point, although contradictory, I was allowed to place Doris Day on her lead whenever Sabine decided it was appropriate. This was achieved by Sabine shouting up the field to me, explaining that Doris behaved better for me than for her.

Our first culinary delight is a *brochette*. A *brochette* is a term used in French cuisine for food cooked on skewers, normally grilled. Our offering is by no means cooked but was indeed on a skewer. It consists of cubes of melon, cherry tomatoes and pieces of frankfurter sausages placed alternately on the stick. Of course, it is served with the obligatory glass of wine, Rose or Red and accompanied by a Vendeen trio singing anti British songs, much to the charign of the nice serving lady, the songs not the wine.

Sabine is not happy. She wants to comprehend how an adult could be served with just one brochette. She is not a child that is appropriate for an infant, not for her.

And so the walk continued with Bill, Becky and myself, reclaiming Doris Day with Sabine subsequently releasing her. This performance went on until at some point Doris Day got so far in front of us that we could not recapture her and decided, even though we had been in a heated altercation with a van owner, who just avoided colliding with her, that she was not our responsibility and quite frankly we gave up.

This section of the *rando* is about five kilometres and apart from getting tired I was also a bit hungry and looking forward to the next eating point which is at *La Chapelle Notre-Dame de Garreau*, of which our house was once the presbytery.

As we walked down the lane to the *Chapelle*, Bill, Becky, Sylvia and myself, with Sabine and John bringing up the rear, some way back, we espied Doris Day down by the tables and were able to call her to us and Becky slipped the lead around her neck. By this time we were at the table to collect our next course, which is *carrottes râpées.* Carrottes râpées is grated carrots with a light dressing, not exactly substantial.

As we lined up to collect this wonderful *repas* placed in plastic containers, one of the ladies serving looked at me with clear hostility and said in precise, formal, French:

"Your dog is a menace. It has been running around the tables and going in the bins," she growled. This aggressive statement was delivered with a contemptuous look which I recognised as the *'les anglais'* stance and that along with the anti-British songs at the last stop, should have made me a little uncomfortable but it had the effect of making me a touch feisty.

I looked her back full in the eye and replied in my best correct French, "It is not my dog."

At this point she did look a bit nonplussed and not surprisingly really, because she could have been forgiven for thinking Doris is my dog as I had spent the best part of the last nine kilometres chasing her around the vendeen countryside.

With a great deal of dignity and a little bit of suspicion in her voice, she demanded with profound authority, "Well, who's it then?"

The timing was impeccable, I could not have planned it better. Sabine is at that very moment wielding her considerable bulk and aura towards the serving table, whereupon, I pointed towards her and declared, "It's hers."

"Oh, what a lovely dog," replied the turncoat.

I should have left the *rando* at that point on a high note with the utterance of that classic line but, no, fool that I am I felt honour bound to complete it.

I am not a carrot fan to be fair and only managed a couple of mouthfuls. I cannot repeat what Sabine though of this feast! However, instead of a single glass of wine to accompany the course, there were several bottles of wine on each trestle table and we copiously imbued this unlooked for treat, all except Sylvia that is, who does not drink alcohol.

The next two stages of the *rando* were the shortest ones, thank goodness, and were centred around the village. By now, because we are not the quickest of walkers, it was starting to turn to dusk and many of the other participants were eating their main course or desert at the remaining feeding points and so halfway through the third section, we had to consult our map. Even with this consultation we did go a little wrong but I believe that was because our orienteering skills were slightly affected by the amount of wine we had drunk.

We finally reached our third destination in the garden behind the *retrait* (retirement home) for old and retired priests and queued up along with the other stragglers for our main course. This feast consists of *jambon et mogettes.* Jambon in this context is a thick slice of bacon cooked like gammon, along with another plastic container containing *mogettes* (a vendeen delicacy), which are basically white beans, like baked beans but without the tomato sauce. Along with this is served our cheese course, which is a piece French stick along with a wrapped wedge of camembert cheese.

Now it has to be said that Sabine is quite a large woman with an appetite to match and this 'gourmet' meal as it had been promoted is not entirely fulfilling her expectations. This is not helped by the fact she hates *mogettes.* I did offer her my cheese wedge and the kind serving lady did say that she could have an extra slice of *jambon* instead of the beans if she wanted, but both of these olive branches were point blank refused. Oh, dear, thank goodness there are bottles of wine on the table and not just a glass. Another positive is that a tethered Doris Day is laid nicely underneath the table, tied to a trestle leg by her lead.

"12 euros for this shit," thundered Sabine.

Oh, dear.

"All I need now is the dessert to be apple pie and my happiness will be complete." She hissed sarcastically. "I hate apple pie."

Oh, dear.

Sabine was then consumed by an enormous sulking period, no words were to be uttered by her and she seemed to have lost the power of hearing.

Sylvia on realising the latter affliction utilised the situation and Sabine's condition to utter uncomfortably under her breath in hushed tones, "I came on this last year and it was apple pie."

What you came back again for this and with no alcohol?

So, a dejected group of walkers reluctantly left the penultimate *rando* stage. I was more than tempted by just remaining where I was and draining as many bottles of wine as I could procure and so I think was Bill. However, the pull of just finishing the damn thing is stronger and so we set off five very apprehensive English folk and one very sulky, hungry French person.

The last stage feeding point is literally around the corner at the *Salle de Polyvalente* (which means multi-purpose hall), so we really did not have time to contemplate the pudding saga. By the time we arrived it was dark and tables have been erected outside the hall in rows, the beverage on offer is different types of tea. I thought this was a little odd, considering people had not exactly been pro-English on the walk. There is not a coffee pot in sight. I politely declined the offer of tea and unwisely sat next to Sabine to await the serving *à table* of the last course, dessert. And so it arrived *Tarte Tatin,* a variation with a caramel base of Apple Pie.

None of us said a word.

Sabine stood up and without uttering a single word, located Doris and waved goodbye. I think it was a wave and then she silently left.

I will not be going next year, even if a can have red wine fed intravenously and I do not think Sabine will be asking me!

Tuesday, 7 August

What the hell are the rules for Boules? I have absolutely no idea.

When I was a child of about 11 or 12, I used to play Crown Green Bowling in Coleshaw Green Park, an unusual pastime for one so young but that was how I rolled, excuse the pun. I grasped the rudiments quite quickly, you had several woods, so called because traditionally they were made of that material and you rolled these bowls in turn towards a small ball called a 'jack' that someone had previously sent along the green diagonally with the intention of getting your bowls as close to it as possible. This French boule lark is not the same. Firstly, the balls are made of metal and the jack is called a *Cochonnet* (piglet), traditionally this equipment would be for the game *Petanque*, but the locals called this activity boules, very confusing. Secondly, the balls are sort of thrown crossed dropped towards the piglet with the same intention as the

English version of getting as many as close as you can to win the game. Further confusion is caused, well, for me, in determining the order in which you throw your balls. There does not seem to be any, either that or Sabine just makes it up as we go along.

During the four major weeks of the French summer holidays, customarily the last two weeks of July and the first two weeks of August, the village campsite *Les Ouches de Jaunay* organises a Boules Tournament each Tuesday evening. It is arranged for the holiday makers staying on the site but is well attended by the locals from Martinet. The process is that each team has two people who play two other people in a single match. If you win the match, you buy the 'losers' a drink. There are approximately eight matches throughout the evening, so if you are not very proficient in the game, you can end up being extremely drunk at the end of the competition and definitely not out of pocket.

The first time I attended the tournament was not very successful. Sabine arrived as usual at my house and told me I would be attending the campsite that evening. It was so much easier to agree, so I did. Apparently, my partner is 'Annie'. I had never met her before in my life and Sabine would partner Giles, I had met him once. One evening Sabine had arrived at the gate and asked (very unusual) if Giles could look around the house. I had no idea who this Giles was or indeed where he was, but as always with the majority of Sabine's requests (commands), I acquiesced and suddenly as if by magic Gilles appeared from behind Sabine like a rabbit out of a hat, which did rather startle me and gave me an overwhelming urge to giggle. Sabine then proceeded to give him a guided tour of the whole house without any help or permission from me, completing the visit with the closing question, "Do you like it?"

Giles gave the request due consideration and replied, "Yes, but it doesn't have enough land."

Piss off.

It was agreed (well, I was told) that Annie would pick me up in her car and take me up to the campsite and Sabine would transport Giles there on her yellow scooter. I could not understand why I could not just walk up the road but that did not seem to be an option, so as usual I conceded and Annie arrived near enough on time and off we went. It turned out that Annie is actually Mum to the opinionated Giles and they had arrived together from *Saint Jean de Monts*. Why Giles had been dropped off at Sabine's is beyond my comprehension but quite frankly, I did not ask. We had just got into the first game, which I think I was doing okay at but not knowing any of the rules that might not have been the case, when the heavens opened and we had to run for shelter. It was agreed by the campsite management after it persisted to rain that the tournament was cancelled.

Oh.

It was then agreed by the Sabine management team, that herself, Giles and Annie would all come back to mine.

Oh.

The night turned out as expected. There was a lot of music played, lots of conversation which I did actually understand the majority of as Annie and Giles spoke a fair amount of English and an inordinate amount of alcohol drunk. It was not so much the amount, as the beer and red wine that is drunk at the many impromptu *soirees* is always substantial but it was the quantity of Jack Daniels imbued by the designated driver Annie. I am glad I was not with her for that leg of the journey.

So, tonight is Tuesday and Sabine arrived on cue this morning and announced that we would be going to play boules that evening. I did not even try to argue. It was going to be different tonight though she said as her partner Gabrielle had arrived from Paris for her two-week *vacances* and she would be coming along. This did not bode well, Sabine as well as being extremely bossy is also excruciatingly honest and had told me previously that Gabrielle did not like me and also, they had had 'disputes' about me. I drank and danced too much apparently, the fact that this dancing and drinking was also with Mr C and not just Sabine did not seem to have any bearing on the matter, ooops.

I said, "Okay." I would meet them all up at the campsite as John was attending also.

"No, I will come and collect you and I will take you up on my scooter," Sabine declared.

"No, no, it is good. I will walk," I reasoned in my best French.

"No, I will take you."

Oh, for God's sake, it was only up the road, so I tried again.

"You take Gabrielle and I will walk."

"No, she can walk. I will take you."

Sabine would convey me safely up the couple of hundred yards to the campsite and her love interest who she had not seen for two months would have to walk.

Well, if the woman did not like me before, then she definitely would not after this.

At the designated time Sabine arrived on her scooter, carrying an extra crash helmet, Gabrielle's I presume, and off we went. As the scooter wobbled constantly due to the large wooden box secured behind the passenger seat, a receptacle for Doris Day not a Pizza Carrying Box as previously thought, I had to grab hold of Sabine around the waist. And so, we arrived at the campsite in that fashion, Gabrielle was already there.

I prayed that my partner for the tournament would be John and the two lovebirds would be the other team, but, oh, no, of course that is not the case. I am to be Sabine's partner.

Oh, dear.

We had varying success in the ensuing games. I think we won as many as we lost, so the drink buying budget levelled out over the night. I am still none the wiser of when I should throw my boule. It seemed to be that sometimes we all went in order, sometimes I threw all of mine one after another or a variation of the two. And for some unknown reason I am always the person who has to throw the piglet. I do not know if that is because I am the shortest and so Sabine thought I would not send it as far as the others would. On no occasion could I ascertain any correlation between the turns of throwing and what is happening in the game.

I was fully conscious throughout though of Gabrielle's presence and did have a bit of a hairy moment when Sabine insisted on buying me a drink (this was extra to the win/lose purchase) and not for her love but I drew the line when she tried to add a sweet crepe to the order.

When the night came to a close, I set off walking towards the lake homewards. This was not to be allowed.

"I will take you home," announced Sabine.

For goodness' sake.

"No, I walk," (I cannot do the tenses, subjective etc) I replied with authority.

"No, I will take you," was the response.

That did not work then.

"You go with Gabrielle," I reasoned while smiling at Gabrielle to try and somehow reassure her I was not after her woman.

"She can wait here; I will take you and then return."

Bollocks!

Cats Can Swim

Monday, 13 May

I really wanted to talk about vibrators, not that I am a fully paid-up member of a sex toy interest group, I want you to know but I would much prefer talking about dildos than being stuck up a corner for two hours with Brenda crying and moaning. She is a funny woman to say the least and why she feels that I am the person to listen to all her woes is beyond me, considering the way she has treated me since we came here.

The first time I met Brenda was shortly after we arrived here. Susan and Richard kindly asked us around to their house to meet the 'English', who live here permanently. There are further '*Anglais*' who have holiday homes but they tend to start to arrive in the spring. So there was myself and Mr C, Susan and Richard, Joyce and Brian and Brenda and Gerald, Emmanuelle and Mark were not attending, the way this was said was a little mysterious.

I had decided how to dress before I went. I did not want to be over exuberant. I was in a little village in the countryside after all. I was glad I did dress down a tad as it was all just a little bit steady. It is strange that just because you are English does not mean that you have anything in common with your fellow country men and women other than your language. I like Susan and Richard; Joyce is very nice but would not have been in my circle of friends in the UK. Brian is a male chauvinist of the first rank. Brenda is very strange and Gerald is uncannily like Frank out of The Vicar of Dibley.

I did not see any of them again other than Susan and Richard for several months, then in June, Susan asked if I wanted to be 'a lady who lunches'. Susan was going to introduce me to other 'permanent' residents from neighbouring villages, excellent. As usual I considered what to wear, which turned out to be totally inappropriate as Susan remarked when she saw me. "You will be boiling in those!"

She is correct. I have just not got used to the climate yet.

Brenda had said that she would pick me up along with Joyce, very kind of her and then collect Susan on route to the restaurant. Brenda arrived at the allotted time and as I walked out to meet the car on the drive, I was extremely conscious of my appearance being closely scrutinised by the two ladies seated in the front of the vehicle. I smiled sweetly and made to get in the back of the car.

I had only got one foot in the door before Brenda stated irritably, "Put your seat belt on."

I was a little taken aback, under normal circumstances with regular friends I would have said something like "Keep your hair on, I'm coming" but on this occasion I just carried on smiling sweetly while making a mental note that this woman was a tad weird. The lunch was good, even though I was melting like a bowl of ice cream and I met two new ladies who both seemed very nice and good fun, thank goodness. Brenda, however, remained quite strange throughout the whole proceedings and I was a little relieved to be deposited without ceremony outside our house.

I was a bit surprised then when I was invited around to Brenda's and Gerald's house for a meal. Mr C was away in the UK and Brenda thought I would be lonely and would I like to join them, which was very considerate. I could not make this woman out, one minute she behaved as though I was a complete interloper from Mars and then the next was inviting me around for an intimate meal. Off I went a little cautiously, I have to admit. It would be nice to be with people for an evening and also, I did think that if I declined that, it would be a massive black mark for me. It turned out to be a quite uneventful evening, not raucous but not unpleasant.

And so, this is how it goes, in company she is very spiky with me but on her own 'turf' she is completely different. I cannot figure her out. Some enlightenment was found when I learned why Emmanuelle did not attend our welcome meal. It was because of Brenda, Oh. It appears that Brenda concentrates on a particular person. At the moment it is Joyce, and then she makes them the centre of her attention until the other person either puts up with it or feels totally smothered and falls out with her. Emmanuelle and Lydia are of the latter. The funny thing is she is not doing that with me but this strange love me hate me hot and cold strategy.

She has continued to invite me around intermittently for meals and always extends the invitation to Mr C. Normally he is in the UK for these occasions but even if he is not, he is not keen to go to say the least, however, it has come to a point when it would be very rude and extremely obvious if he did not attend with me and so off we went. We made a kind of pact before we went that we would just drink lots and have fun, whether they joined in or not, and we did helped enormously by the home brewed *Lemonchello* made by the surprisingly resourceful Gerald. Unfortunately, this has resulted in Mr C being decidedly drunk and I have had to act as a ditch avoiding guide to the very wobbly, weaving, singing husband on the route home.

I had noticed quite early on in our unusual relationship that Brenda liked to tell Gerald what to do, sometimes directly and at others via a roundabout questioning technique.

"Oh, that's a good idea, Gerald, isn't it?" or "Yes, we should do that, Gerald, shouldn't we?"

So, it is with no surprise when my current visit came to a close that Brenda stated nonchalantly, "I think the dogs could do with a walk, couldn't they?" Code for you need to walk our guest home.

"They have had one," came the response.

Brenda looked at him with that, you are silly, you are a bit slow on the uptake look and said, "They probably need another."

"No, they don't."

Oh, dear. Brenda looked a little nonplussed at this answer and decided to go for full command mode. "Our guest needs walking home."

"The lights are on," came the response.

I need to explain at this point about the lights in the village. There are some lamp posts placed strategically around, not on every street but in the main places of thoroughfare or on the '*Lotissments*', a sort of estate. As it happens, Brenda and Gerald's abode is next to such a place and therefore has illumination outside, however, no matter where the streetlights are placed. They are all switched off for the night at 23.00.

At this point after looking at Brenda's 'stroppy/embarrassed' face and Gerald's 'I'm not shifting from this chair face', I felt that I needed to step in before a full-blown domestic incident took place, so I smiled and said, "I'm a big girl, I can walk myself home."

I do not know what the village thought of my journey home tonight as unfortunately, once I had left the confines of Brenda and Gerald's 'rue', there are no lights at all. I cannot stress how dark it is and I do not have a torch or my phone with me. What ensued is the fast clip clopping of my heels on the middle of the tarmacked road to avoid any ditches, interspersed with screams, followed swiftly by giggles, when not one but two owls in separate trees took affront to my noisy return and flew out at me squawking or whatever owls do.

I have never been invited back after that, not because of my raucous shenanigans but for some other random reason.

It all started with the fact that Brenda has 'fallen out' with Joyce, which seemed to be what happened to everyone whom Brenda focused her full attention on. Joyce had apparently taken one of our Dutch neighbours to the delight that is Noz. Noz is a shop like no other I have ever seen, the best way to describe it is like a church jumble sale in the 1960s. It is laid out with rows and rows of trestle tables, mounted on top of which are shallow shelf like appendages into which a variety of random, bizarre and downright strange articles are placed for sale to the general public. Ladies' bras, next to hammers, adjacent to porcelain money boxes, adjoining cheesy puffs, next to plastic beach sandals and so forth. When I visited, I could not find any logical link between any of the items displayed, maybe that is the connection that they have none.

It transpires that Brenda has taken distinct umbrage at Joyce taking our neighbour to this wonderful, slightly bonkers shop. Brenda takes the new people of the village to Noz, not Joyce.

For goodness' sake.

What has any of this to do with me? Nothing.

However, it appears that Brenda has decided I have said something about her to someone else and will not speak to me.

What?

I saw Joyce the other day and the subject got on to Brenda and her decidedly unusual behaviour and Joyce said, "Well, that day we went to lunch for the first time when we came to pick you up, she asked me if I was going to be your friend."

What! Are we five?

Tuesday, 9 April

Ghosts do not exist according to a recent study by UK psychologists. A chill in the air, low light conditions or even magnetic fields are what are responsible for feelings of a presence and in fact are just that feelings, definitely not ghouls, ghosts or your dead gerbil paying you a visit.

Well, they want to come and spend some time in this house then, especially tonight.

After living for a while in France, you come to realise and this is a generalisation I am aware that the French as a nation is very sensible and are governed on the whole by formal processes and procedures. This is quite evident in their treatment of Halloween. The nearest thing you can get to an affirmation that the long departed walked the earth. Halloween is a relatively new thing in France and celebrating it started in the '90s, I suppose at a similar time as in the UK, and now observing Halloween in France has now become fashionable and the 'in' thing.

The French have traditionally celebrated the Catholic holiday of *La Toussaint*, All Saints Day, which falls on 1 November. It is a sad day, where people go back to visit the cemeteries where their dead are interred, clean the tombs, pray and lay flowers, chrysanthemums and then have a family meal. The few weeks on the run up to *La Toussaint,* or 'dead day' as we have irreverently come to call it, supermarkets and garden centres are bursting at the seams with every conceivable colour of these blooms. There is always a brisk trade in these plants and because they are associated with the dead, do not buy them as a gift for the living or else they will think you believe they are ready to leave this mortal coil. I always presumed there was some other significance to the chrysanthemum being the plant of choice for this sombre occasion but it turns out to be a very practical reason for their selection. They happen to be in bloom at the right the time of the year.

It is strange that some sort of Halloween type of activity is not associated in France with All Saints Day as the tradition of dressing up is linked to the medieval practices of mumming, which meant dressing up in costumes, singing, dancing, play-acting and making other general mischief. However, I do not think on reflection this equates on an even level to the type of endeavour associated with *La Toussaint*, although some people will tell you that it is a Celtic celebration that has been observed in Brittany for centuries. In general, Halloween is nothing that reached the general public in the rest of France. Until the '90s that is, where the eminently sensible French thought it was a great opportunity to teach some English words to children.

French children start to learn English in the juniors or elementary school as it is known in France. They cannot have a fluent conversation but as kids the world over they would do anything for sweeties and the opportunity to dress up in a costume parade going trick or treating is too big an opportunity to ignore. So instead of pockets of children roaming the street in the dark, cold evening, chaperoned by the obligatory parent, French children go on mass from school in the daytime with their teachers. It has to be said that it never gets to tricking though because most French homes will not have the stock of confectionary awaiting the little darlings and would be absolutely furious if their houses got toilet papered. So, it works on a kind of appointment system where willing households have been identified and coerced beforehand, presenting a very ordered and well-planned celebration. I did not understand this and waited all day, sweets at the ready for any would be Trick or Treat callers and as you would expect saw none.

I do not know if my neighbours or fellow villagers believe in ghosts but they certainly seem to believe in fables or miracles or more correctly will repeat them at any opportunity, whether or not they feel they a true reflection of the truth is another matter. One such story is that a young child of around ten years old, who was deaf and dumb from birth and was tending her flock when in the middle of the *Lac de Jaunay* on a large stone a beautiful lady appeared. The beautiful lady beckoned to her and said, "Child, do you give me the whitest of your lambs?"

The child replied, "Willingly, beautiful lady, if my mother would agree, I will give you my lamb." Her mother on hearing her daughter speak was so delighted by this miracle of goodness that she said that the lady should have all the sheep in thanks. When they returned to the lake there was just the stone.

Now unless said, beautiful lady was an Olympic swimmer she has got to be a ghost but I suppose the UK psychologists would have a logical explanation. It was a trick of the light, no one was there in the first place and the child regained her speech and hearing through a rare medical anomaly.

What about smell? I do not mean the child or the beautiful lady smelt but what if you start to smell things.

It all started when Mr C began staying away for 11 days at a time, so instead of returning to France every weekend, he returned every other, having three days here before returning to the UK to work for the remaining eleven. He always leaves at about 17.15 on a Sunday evening and although I am quite robust that first night always seems a bit horrendous, I always have a little weep, not so that he can see me and I always but always have quite a bit to drink, my excuse being that it will help me sleep, seeing that it is the first night in the bed on my own. When I retire to bed, I always shut all the doors, I think subconsciously I believe that if someone is in the house and has to open all the doors to get to me, I will hear them. What I would do if this ever happens, I have no idea, and how I would deal with said someone I have not got a clue but it helps me sleep. Therefore, on each Monday morning, I go down the stairs, put the kettle on and open the doors into the lounge, enter and open the curtains.

That first Monday morning Mr C started his fortnightly stint was when I smelt it. It was trumps, that is the only way I can describe it. Now people will say, well, there is a drain nearby or the sink in the kitchen is blocked or some such plumbing issue and I have to say that initially that is what I thought. That was until the following Monday fortnight where upon entering the lounge I smelt cigarette smoke. Now neither myself or Mr C smoke and none of our friends or family smoke in the house, plus no one had been around, so I was a little puzzled but I soon forgot about it until the next Monday fortnight. When I entered the lounge on that occasion, it smelt of body odour and I can say hand on heart it is not myself of Mr C who has that issue. It began to dawn on me that this smelliness only happened on a Monday fortnight and this continued to be the case over several months, not always in sequence. I might have several occasions of trumps, then Body Odour and then smoke and vice versa, however, cigarette smoke did seem to be the most frequent contributor.

I decided that it must be something connected to the house itself. I do not know why that thought came into my head but it came. I did some research and spoke to Giles and Sophie, now I say spoke, I tried to have a conversation with them but in honesty, I only really gleaned a quarter of the information they were imparting to me. I asked them if they knew anything about the history of our house. It is about 150 years old, so it must have some and it appears that as a child Giles lived next door. Excellent. However, what I learned from the rest of the conversation was that Giles hated priests.

Oh.

He also hated wearing his Sunday shoes which he carried to the end of the lane and swapped them with his preferred footwear of choice, clogs and then walked along the main road to church, leaving the said clogs to await his return after the service. I did get a little sidetracked here as I was quite curious to see if it was only himself that performed this change and learned it was the whole village of church goers and so I was fascinated by the thought of all these wooden shoes laid alongside the road. They must have had some kind of system in place, otherwise people would go home with the wrongs one, maybe they did. Were they all honest or did some steal an extra pair? These at the time were interesting questions which were never voiced or answered and were not really providing me with the information I sought. I did find out, however, that on the occasion Giles was discussing they went to *La Chapelle Gareau* not the other church at the top of the village.

Folklore has it that a knight of the middle-ages had tarried too long in a castle in the area and on his way home found that a storm had swollen the waters of the *Jaunay* into tumultuous rapids. He tried to get through, however, his poor horse lost all purchase in the torrent and they started to drift. The knight was afraid and made a vow to the Mighty Mother of the Saviour that if he and his horse made it through alive, he would build a shrine to her, Mary. At this point the same big stone that seems to live in the middle of the *Jaunay* rose out of the water and acted as some kind of pontoon and floated the knight and his steed safely to the banks of the lake. The knight honoured his promise and built the shrine, *La Chapelle Gareau.* Now this does seem to disagree with the official historical version, which says the Chapel was built around

456AD by people wanting to Christianise the local pagans but this is what happens with Legends. They become a bit confusing. The existing building that is there now was built in the 1700s after the previous construction had burnt down.

But what does this have to do with our house, and the ongoing smelly vision?

To be fair it is not just smelling, there is the music. I have lost count of the number of times I have come running into answer the phone in the lounge to find that when I got there, it is silent. Not unusual until I did 3103, the equivalent in France for 1471 to find no call had been made. I did think it a little strange or that I was hearing things but I just carried on with whatever I had been doing until one morning I awoke and as I was laid in bed wondering whether I should get up or not the most unusual thing happened. From the corner of my bedroom came what I can only describe as a Gregorian chant. Now I am not an avid church goer, although I did go to Sunday school when I was a child but I was definitely brought up as Church of England and had never even set foot in a Roman Catholic Church sermon. However, I knew what it was as soon as I heard it, bizarre. I just laid there staring at the corner, thinking what the hell is going on.

The following weekend Mr C was still in England and my nephew's wife, Steph, who also lived in France, a lot of her time on her own with her two daughters asked me if I wanted see Dominque sing. Well, I would love to hear her sing but the last two occasions I have tried to witness this event, Steph had got the wrong location or the wrong date. No, she was quite sure it was this Saturday night at *Cote et Bistrot* in *Saint Gilles Croix de Vie*. So off we went, not as it turns out to enjoy an outstanding performance from the elegant, sophisticated

Dominique, but were witness to a very surreal piece from a trio whose most unusual member looked like the love child of the eighties pop group Sparks.

Steph decided that she would sleep over at ours as the girls were staying with friends, so after a nightcap, she settled herself in the studio and I went off to bed. In the morning I was doing the usual lying in bed, wondering whether to get up or not when I heard the music again, but because I was laid down and not moving around, I could hear it better and could analyse it a bit more. It sounded like choir music. When I went downstairs, I went through the motions of checking the phone but as usual there had been no call. When Steph wandered into the lounge for a coffee before heading off to pick the girls up, I asked, "Did your mobile phone ring?"

Steph replied, "You mean the music? I heard that."

Well, at least I was not going mad and not the only one hearing things.

Why was it all happening? I had no idea but a chance meeting with an American lady, who lives in the next village gave me some indication. It turns out this lady is a landscape gardener and used to be the nanny to the son of the previous but one owners of our house and she had designed their garden from scratch. They had bought the house when it was just one building and a pig shed (the now studio), had renovated it, put the pool in etc. They had bought it from the church and up until the sale, it had been the presbytery for *La Chapelle Gareau*.

Well, in my head everything is now making sense, apparently the last priest who lived in the presbytery was infirm and only lived in the downstairs part of the house. He had died and each church in the district no longer had a dedicated priest but operated on a kind of 'priest pool' system and so as a consequence, they had decided to sell the building to raise some well needed funds. When Giles said he did not like priests, he meant those living next door, not the priesthood in general.

I settled into a sort of routine and viewed my 'priest' as a kind influence who was keeping an 'eye' on me. I decided after the umpteen time of picking the key up off the floor in the back bedroom after I had securely placed it in the keyhole to just remove it altogether. And after I had found my lovely 'chambre' sign from off the door of that same bedroom halfway down the stairs after numerous efforts to practically superglue it back on, I still thought 'he' is looking after me but just did not wanting anything in or on that door.

The problem is if I was to tell anyone these things, they, which I had not, would think I was mad and raving. Except that is for Mr C, he believes me, but he does not count. However, tonight, other people are here witness to some very strange goings on in the lounge.

It had become our habit, Emmanuelle, Lydia, Susan and myself, to have a 'ladies' night' about once every month. This consisted of a nice meal, copious amounts of alcohol and was where we set the world to rights until the next time. I never asked Brenda again after being trapped in a corner of the lounge for two hours with a wailing, weeping weirdo. It usually took place at our house as invariably I did not have a husband hanging around. Tonight is no different; we get so tied up in discussing anything and everything to the nth degree that we do not even move away from the table. While we were generally sorting all the ills of the world and character assassinating quite a few people (some of whom were locals), we were listening to Robbie Williams. I say listening it is more background music actually and it was quite some time before we realised old Robbie had stopped his crooning and the CD player was quietly waiting to be reloaded with another one from the collection.

Then it happened.

All of a sudden, the phone started making peculiar noises – it was like someone had picked up the receiver and was dialling out, but that there was a lot of interference and they were definitely not going to get through on that line. The problem is that the phone is still in the cradle. We had all stopped mid-sentence and looked towards the handset in a mixture of annoyance, curiosity and intrigue, our heads cocked to one side like a group of Labradors. Simultaneously the phone stopped and our friend Robbie began to sing again – not the first song on the album, but the second. Curious. He sang and completed his song and the CD player fell silent for the second time. Nothing.

We looked at each other with a mixture of expressions. Lydia and Susan are very curious and open minded to what is going on; Emmanuelle on the other hand looked a little concerned, whereas I am quite excited that something is happening while other people are here. I did not disclose my 'priest theory' and let the three of them debate the various synopses they came up with, which I have to say are all of the paranormal variety, strangely enough. We carried on thus, drinking and laughing, the concept and conjecture getting wilder and wilder the more alcohol we consumed, until it happened again.

Emmanuelle was off; she had her coat on and she was out the door.

Thursday, 27 June

"Recherché une personne responsable pour s'occuper d'une fille de quatre ans pendant deux semaines en août. Les taux de rémunération normaux s'appliquent."

This was a notice stuck to the counter in the shop; it said, roughly translated, "Wanted: responsible person to take care of a four-year-old girl for two weeks in August. Normal rates of pay apply."

"I can do that," I said as I jabbed the piece of paper, quite violently actually, with my finger.

Emmanuelle looked a little startled at first but followed the trajectory of my finger and replied with a simple "Yes".

"I could do," I reiterated.

"Yes, I know you could. Do you want me to ring her?"

"Oh yes, please." I enthused.

The telephone is a bit of a problem for me it has to be said; when you are trying to speak in a language that is not your mother tongue it is so much simpler to be able to speak face to face and then the awkward silences and inevitable mistakes can be easily covered with hand gestures and innovative miming. Not so on the phone.

Emmanuelle said that she would call the number and then ring me back, which she did within the hour. The lady in question would like to see me. Emmanuelle had explained I was English, had experience looking after children etc. and would like to help, and so Madam asked for me to go around at 16.45.

I do not know why I am so nervous walking up the road and around the corner the few hundred yards; everywhere is easy to find in Martinet – it is only two weeks child minding, for goodness sake.

I arrived at the address that I had scribbled down from Emmanuelle and realised that I had passed by before with the dogs when the residents were having some sort of party, probably a housewarming as it was a new bungalow, and very nice it looked too. I rang the bell and waited in trepidation. I need not have worried. Madam, Sonia, is lovely – in her thirties I would say. She explained, well I think she did, that she had spoken to a young girl who lived across the road but she was not certain she was old enough to look after her daughter (either she was being overprotective or her daughter was a bit of a 'madam' herself) and she was seeing another lady later that day. She took my telephone number and said she would let me know, tricky.

Off I went home for a large glass of red.

The next day at about 10.00 in the morning, the phone rang; I answered it and was greeted by the voice of a man, speaking in French. Oh no, I was a little perturbed, and as my telephone French is hesitant at best and incoherent at worse, I did my utmost to understand what was being said and hopefully give the correct responses, which I am not totally convinced that I did. On the phone was "Monsieur" to Madam from yesterday and he was a little concerned about my ability to look after his daughter and would like to meet me. Nothing if not honest. He was going to come around at 10.45. There was no negotiation on his part – just command, and on mine just acquiesce and so I awaited with apprehension for his arrival.

At the appointed time there was the ring on the bell. I opened the gate and was a little surprised, as there before me was the gentleman in question accompanied by a girl of about 14 and the object of my interview, the little girl herself. JP, as I have learnt is his name, shook my hand while saying hello and introduced his two daughters, Julienne who is 12 and Clea who is 4. Both kissed me, as is usual for children when greeting adults in France, and Clea handed me a drawing she had done especially for me, so I crouched down, thanked her and kissed her again.

JP stayed for 45 fraught minutes; not for him because he just spoke to me as normal, but I was desperately trying to follow what he was saying, play the hostess and try to entertain the girls as well. JP's main concern was the language issue and how this would impact on my care of Clea, Clea appeared to have no such concerns and we were fast becoming good friends. JP was concerned that Clea was a bit 'turbulent'. Oh, what a good word to describe her, but I tried to allay his fears by telling him about my children and grandchildren. I think that is what I had told him because after he had repeated about ten times his worry about language, he agreed that I was the ideal person and asked if I could also look after Julienne when his and Sonia's shifts coincided – meaning she would be left at home for more than three hours. Yes, of course. JP and Sonia both work at an establishment for disabled adults and children. I think they are both physiotherapists, but I might be wrong about that – my understanding about that is a little shaky. So, it was arranged that Sonia would give me the dates and times over the two-week period when I would be looking after the girls and as they left, Clea flung her arms around my waist and hugged me violently; I think she likes me.

Oh my god.

I admit that I have pursued the child-minding 'job' because I am missing my own grandchildren and I thought that it would help fill the 'gap'; also as the time goes on, I realise that I also want to help Sonia as a working mum.

For the past three summers I have looked after Clea; the first time I had Julienne as well, but after that initial time she felt too old to have to have someone look after her. The first season I got the standard 'pay' but since then it has been less and sometimes, like when I have her while they go to Julienne's parents evening, I accept no payment. I suppose I am trying to act as a surrogate grandparent, but to be honest it is not the same, I am more like an eccentric aunt.

I say 'was' because all that has stopped now. I have had Clea for the last three summers but no more; the lure of '*Mamie*' and 'proper' swimming lessons has beaten me hands down and if I am honest, I am a little relieved, as she is more than a little 'turbulent'.

We have had some interesting moments over the years – like when Steve was meandering past the swimming pool and she decided he need to go in, whereupon she picked him up and threw him without ceremony in the shallow end before I realised what was happening. Well, it turns out cats can swim. I jumped in, which is a shock in itself, pulled the proverbial drowned rat out of the pool, wrapped him in a towel and cuddled him on my knee while telling off a defiant four-year-old in my limited French. Steve sat and purred his head off, stupid cat. She was grounded by her parents from using the 'piscine' on her next sojourn. That is all fine and dandy but you try and entertain a French, belligerent, hard done by toddler with the attention span of a goldfish for three-and-a-half hours when all she wants is to go in the swimming pool!

The swimming pool has featured heavily in Clea's desire to spend her time with me rather than her grandmother. Julienne had quite diplomatically tried to persuade me, however, that her father felt it was not necessary for Clea to wear armbands, a lifejacket and a rubber ring whilst enjoying the delights of the pool. Well, I am sorry but no one is drowning on my watch – maybe the proposed swimming lessons were in direct response to this.

I have to admit that I will not miss her determination to have everything her own way to the point of downright stubbornness, which I know is like all young children but it is very difficult to deal with in a burgeoning foreign language. Neither will I regret having to deal with her very inappropriate behaviour towards my mortified son-in-law on the beach at Grand Plage, or the grabbing, roughly, of mine and Jemima's breasts on the way home in the car.

I will, however, miss her little face and the way she thinks the word 'cushion' is hilarious as it sounds like 'pig' in French, the cuddles and kisses and the fun we have had, but as much as I love her, she is not mine and it is not the same.

Monday, 22 July

I am knackered.

I think it is safe to say that I am getting too old for this.

We have just had all the kids to stay, when I see all that is not entirely not all the children, our two boys and their families have not been. Our eldest boy has visited us previously but I think his holiday tastes now run to 'all inclusive' jaunts in red-hot exotic countries as opposed to a sojourn in the French countryside around a pool. He works hard and only has so many weeks holidays, so if that's what he wants to do, good for him. The youngest son is a different kettle of fish; he only interacts with us around Christmas and his birthday – the rest of the year he seems not to be in 'communication mode', so consequently he has never visited us. So, it was the three girls and their families, 13 of us in total – eight adults, three children and two babies who came.

Oh, my God.

I think I did quite well with the logistics of it all. Jessie and her mob were in the studio; I think they got the best deal there as they had their own bedrooms and bathroom. Daphne and her brood were in our bedroom, a bit like sardines with camp beds and the travel cot strategically fitted in the available space. We were in the back bedroom and Jemima and Mr 'six-foot-two and three quarters' were on a blow up double mattress on the lounge floor with the dogs. The amount of bedding and towels it took to facilitate these arrangements was phenomenal and I even managed to achieve to some level of colour coordination.

Mealtimes were more of a challenge, it has to be said.

The last time they all came, myself and Mr C were in the lounge – which seemed like a sensible and practical option at the time as we would be the people who were locking up etc. It turned out to be a bit of a 'mare'. It was not just the fact that we were sleeping on the floor on a blow-up bed at our age or that one morning I awoke to find Jack in bed with me with his head on my pillow, it was the lack of sleep. It appeared that every night each of the kids took it in turn to get plastered and either drank and drank until the early hours or performed the end scene from *Dirty Dancing* with a great deal of enthusiasm in the middle of the lounge. We all however, got a little squiffy when we had the housewarming party, especially Luke.

John and Maude were returning to the area for the first time and wanted to come and see the house they had sold to us; they were generally being nosey, wanting to see what we had done. It seemed appropriate to have a bit of a get together to facilitate this, so they could meet up with old friends and we could make new ones. Everything went really well, although John and Maud did not stay long and were a bit perturbed that we had had a fence erected around the pool. The party went on into the early hours and people one by one drifted off home or to bed and that just left Susan, Richard, Daphne, Luke, Mr C and myself and a new neighbour we had met – Jane. Her husband had left earlier to go and rescue their daughter who was on route and her car had broken down. Jane decided it was time that she should go and Luke, being the chivalrous person he is, said that he would walk her the short distance home and so they departed. A few minutes later they both appeared back in the garden. Jane had decided that she could not let Luke walk back on his own in the dark and in such a drunken state and so had walked him back home.

The next day was spent a little more sedately than usual for all of us and when Esther popped around for a visit to see them, she found us all laid around the pool and screeched, "It's just like bloody Butlins!"

The reason they are all here this time is that we have sold the house and are going back and so, they have come for their last holiday here.

I began to reflect on why we came to France in the first place. The urge to live abroad was born out of my love of voyeuristic TV, I am not your Big Brother Celebrity Get-Me-

Out-of-Essex type but more A Place in the Sun convert, hence the compulsion. It was partly also because I was accused, quite unfounded I may add, of some kind of nefarious activity; I had been accused of procuring a mobile home by accounting fraud. Now if someone were to ask me if I could and if I was that kind of person, what would I steal? After long deliberation and consideration, I do not think that a caravan would come high on that imaginary list. It is not that I think there is anything wrong with caravans, I am sure they are very nice vehicles, in fact my sister had one for years.

It is more, well, a question of ego and reputation really. If someone is going to accuse me of embezzlement, I would hope that I would procure something a little more elaborate than a caravan, for God's sake. If I was willing to risk imprisonment and professional humiliation, I would go for something a tad more unique and imaginative than a bloody winnebago! It is like going into Faberge and pinching a radio-controlled alarm clock.

I have never even wanted a caravan. With the size of our family it would have to be huge to even accommodate half of us. To be honest my hopes and dreams ran more to owning a foreign holiday home somewhere warm, not a camper van.

So, after the appalling and unfounded accusation of my criminal activity and 'Campergate', we decided that we were going to follow the latest fantasy and buy a place abroad. I am not saying that the act of being accused of stealing made me think 'Oh let's get a holiday home', but it was the trigger that set it in motion along with both our redundancy money.

Socrates said, "It is not living those matters but living rightly."

I agree but I think I would rather use the words from a 1998 romantic comedy, *Hope Floats,* "Beginnings are scary, endings are usually sad, but it's the middle that counts the most."

I do not think that the screen writer who penned that particular line was a great philosopher, I may be wrong, but I think that he or she is correct. We have had the beginning, middle and are now at the end and it is incredibly sad, but there is something else in there too.

There have been times that I have been astounded at the differences between France and the UK; I think this is because as a person I believe myself to be cultured, tolerant and a little bit sophisticated and do not want to sound prejudiced against other cultures. I have to admit that I utter statements such as, "Oh, we are not all that different" and "We are all the same. We just speak a different language" – I must sound like a right arrogant twonk sometimes.

Even I at my most benevolent, annoying, self, I have to admit there are times when you just cannot deny it, there are differences – they just come out of nowhere and leave you gobsmacked.

When we had our first holiday to France as a 'new' family as a research exercise for contemplating moving, on the first day we decided to explore our surroundings and look for somewhere to have an evening meal. As we left the little country lane where our accommodation was situated, we immediately identified the route through the village towards the sea front; it is only a small place so it was quite easy.

As we walked along the main thoroughfare towards the shore, I became a little startled. Well to be honest, at first, I was not sure what I was, because I could not quite believe what I was seeing. It was a little bit like those cartoon characters who overstate the obvious by vigorously rubbing their eyes while subsequently poking them out of their sockets on sticks accompanied by a loud pinging noise. A confused look at Mr C and Jemima confirmed my suspicion that we were all having the same hallucinatory episode. There before us tethered on the grass verge skirting the pavement we were walking on, was a zebra and a monkey. Further investigation revealed other out of context animals such as horses, llamas and more monkeys.

We were astounded. It took some highly animated squealing discussion (the screeching was primarily from myself and Jemima) to conclude that it was not a strange pets' corner but that they were in fact animals belonging to a travelling circus. At one point I thought I had wandered across a parallel universe into *The Wizard of Oz*.

Off we wondered, continuing our journey in quite a quiet reflective mood, interspersed with half-started, never-finished comments like "well…" and "why…" and "what the hell…"

When we arrived still perplexed at the promenade, which was just a small street, we realised that our evening's culinary delight did not reside in the village; there were a couple of places to eat but they were mainly little cafes selling snacks.

So, before we left, we had a walk on the beach and just to put the world back in the right perspective, we had a game of crazy golf. Yes, so very sophisticated.

Never regret; if it is good, it is wonderful; if it is bad, it is experience. So here we are, at the end of the journey.

When we first moved to France, we used to look at the fantastic 'visages' and would say with smugness, "This or the Tesco's roundabout?" No competition.

Who would have thought that Tesco's roundabout would have won??? Trying to use other people's children to fill the massive hole in your heart is not entirely successful. Watchful ghosts, local acceptance and good friends although helpful are not enough, return is inevitable.

HAVING SOMEWHERE TO GO IS HOME
HAVING SOMEONE TO LOVE IS FAMILY
HAVING BOTH IS A BLESSING